There Is No Magic

... BUT THERE ARE ALTERNATIVES TO
PARENTING EXCEPTIONAL CHILDREN

STEPHEN DUBROFSKY M.A., M.Ed.
Educational Therapist
Family Counselor

American Literary Press, Inc.
Five Star Special Edition
Baltimore, Maryland

There Is No Magic

Library of Congress
Cataloging in Publication Data
ISBN 1-56167-815-5

Library of Congress Card Catalog Number:
2003094933

Published by

American Literary Press, Inc.
Five Star Special Edition
8019 Belair Road, Suite 10
Baltimore, Maryland 21236

Manufactured in the United States of America

To my teachers:
Jenna And Chelsea

Table of Contents

THERE IS NO MAGIC

ACKNOWLEDGEMENTS

This is a very special part for me. It signifies an opportunity to say a few words that truly run deep. I wish to thank my good friend Mimi, all of our walks and talks together continue to inspire me in the pursuit and exploration of my personal gifts. Then there is my very good and long time dear friend, John who was the first to read and critique TINM. Thank you for your recommendations on making the title a more focused one. Your support and recognition has been important to me. This time has been special because it has nurtured and grown our friendship. And you Rosy, well what can I say, with an impish smile on my face, we truly are spiritual partners, I relish the times we talk. You continue to teach me about the value of listening, believing and having faith. As Gomer Pyle would say....... THANK YOU.... THANK YOU..... THANK YOU.

And to you Daryl, I don't think you know how important you have been. We have shared much together, you have always been there to talk to when I was having insecure moments, and you have allowed me to support you in your moments. You have and continue to be a wonderful mirror for me.

But of course... then there are you Jenna and Chelsea, two of the greatest daughters any father could ask for, I thank you for being my teacher and truly showing me the way....

Thank you all.

PREFACE

An excerpt from "The Prophet" Kahlil Gibran

Your children are not your children.
They are the sons and the daughters of life's longing for
itself.

They come through you, but not from you
and though they are with you, yet they belong not to you.

You may give them your love, but not your thoughts
for they have their own thoughts.

You may house their bodies, but not their souls
for their souls dwell in the house of tomorrow,
which you cannot visit, not even in your dreams.

You may strive to be like them, but seek not to make
them like you,
for life goes not backward, nor tarries with yesterday.

You are the bows from which your children as living
arrows are sent forth.
The archer sees the mark upon the path of the infinite,
and he bends you with his might that his arrows may go
swift and far.

Let your bending in the archer's hand be for gladness.
For even as he loves the arrow that flies,
so he loves also the bow that is stable.

The Prophet, Kahlil Gibran

There   **Is**   **No**

"M"
    Magic
    Miracle
    Motivation

"A"
    Accomplishment
    Acceptance
    Advocate
    Anxiety
    Awareness

"G"
    Genius
    Gentleness
    Gratitude
    Guide

"I"
    Initiative
    Introspective
    Intuitive

"C"
    Colossal
    Compassion
    Compatibility

Magic? You might ask. What is this thing about magic? There are many parenting books that have been written and most of them presume that if you follow very specific guidelines that your problems will be solved. Within our speedy and technological world, we have attempted to tie things up in neat and tidy packages. We try to make things easy. We know that isn't quite true. The act of bringing up children, especially those that many have an exceptionality, is not like this. To be a parent encompasses everything that has to do with life, as you shall see as you read on.

Magic . . . well the fact is that this word tells us that things may happen from thin air. We love to go see magicians and their tricks, it makes us feel good, we laugh, it peaks our interest. We enjoy the sensations where we are surprised in pleasant ways.

When extraordinary things happen that we can't explain we call them, miracles but are they illusions?

Can we explain how a child is born? Where we come from? How the act of conception leads to this amazing being? Is this magical or an illusion? I think not, this is all real and it is a gift presented to us. We can touch them, feel their tender skin, smell their freshness and hear their wants and desires. Are these beings perfect? Yes they are, as we all know that we are all unique in our own way, no matter what our package looks like.

We become motivators and teachers so that we may pass on what we have learned, as our children are busy growing up and learning who they really are.

Accomplishment, speaks for itself as we acknowledge the act of bringing a new life into the world, wow … really it is time to pat yourselves on the back. Yet during difficult times it is important to accept what is before you, surrender old ideas or ways in favor of learning new and exciting things and opening up doors that will lead to real surprises. As we move through these doors or "Spots" as you will soon read we feel things like anxiety, fear, disappointment and heartbreak. The joy in it all is that we are taking a chance, we are learning more about ourselves, about how to become more effective parents, about how to look at things in different ways and we are becoming more aware and learn the importance of advocating for our children. And OH yes we are truly growing by leaps and bounds and testing new territories by standing up for our children and ourselves. We feel a new sense of self-esteem and are ten feet tall.

Genius is in all of us. If we thought of ourselves as 'geniuses' (which we really are) and nothing else then we would all feel great about ourselves no matter how we are packaged. There would be no labeling, no belittling. That we would begin to understand the feeling that comes along with being gentle to ourselves and others and we would learn to enjoy this practice. Then as we move through different "Spots" we would feel what it is to be grateful for having the opportunity to do this thing we call parenting and I bet we would want to practice this as well. Then all of a sudden as if by some "Magic" we realize that being a parent is not about control or power but about being a guide and a teacher and you would learn to enjoy this as well.

Initiative means to take the bull by the horns, and realize that change is all around us and because of the nature of these educational and social changes that we must take a greater degree of responsibility for the education of our child. We must learn all there is to know about how to provide for their needs and then do whatever is necessary to make sure that this comes true. Is this magic? As we continue the journey along we recognize the benefits of looking inside, this thing that we call introspection we begin to see the power in this and the depth in it all. At this point we also recognize that we must listen to ourselves, what our hearts and minds are telling us of the decision that are required. We call this intuition. Once we are in touch with this then nothing can interfere because we are surely flying along.

Colossal? Yes it may seem that this job is a monumental one, for it truly is. Along the way we have an opportunity to see how compatible we are with ourselves, what type of parenting style we possess and to look at the personality traits and temperament of our children and then adjust it all so that as a family we are all more compatible.

For as we all will learn that it is our **Compassion, Understanding, and Firmness,** that will lead us through any challenge or "Spots".

"There is No Magic" is about the fact that each and everyone of us possess within us all what is required to take care of our children and ourselves and make this a happy, healthy and harmonious life no matter what the circumstances may be.

THIS IS THE MAGIC IN IT ALL

ENJOY . . . . I thank you all for choosing this book; I would love to hear each and every one of your experiences and thoughts about it. I welcome all questions that you may have.

Stephen Dubrofsky

INTRODUCTION

THERE IS NO MAGIC

... But there are alternatives to Parenting Exceptional Children

THERE IS NO MAGIC is about many things that will help you as parents learn more about your special needs child, about yourselves, and about your family as a whole. This material presents the framework for a new way of looking at the way we're currently parenting. A new way, but one still based upon some of the aspects of your existing one. Your current parenting style may be feeling quite ineffective in today's society. It may be one that is creating more dissonance, than harmony. This material will help you to develop an awareness of, and skills for, what your child's needs might be; what your needs are; and how you might deal with issues that you once thought insurmountable. I am not saying that this will be a simple thing, because from experience we know that changing a paradigm hardly ever is. Life may be far too complex to deal with all of the problems, trials and tribulations of having a child with special needs, but we have been given an opportunity here to reassess how we look at things and the chance to make different choices.

This material will talk about how you can be better partners with your children and with their school. It will give you a perspective of what the school can offer and how the style of educating your child has changed. It will offer insight into how you can make your home into a better educational and social environment for your child.

THERE IS NO MAGIC will help to teach you how to assess what the needs of both you and your child are. It will encompass a broad picture that includes the effects of a nutritional program and exercise regime, which can be designed to meet the individual needs of the child. It will supply you the types of assessments required in order to create an educational and social plan that fits your special child's disability. It speaks of how to create a plan for how to best manage and motivate your child. It helps to give you a better understanding of who your child is, how they learn and how they should be taught based upon their individual skills. It talks about your role as a parent. By understanding the behaviors that we bring into the mix as adults, this knowledge can help us to be more effective in managing our child on a daily basis. It speaks of your journey and your feelings of fear, joy, betrayal, and failure as you are faced with the moment-to-moment life responsibility of raising a special needs child.

Through all of this there will be one common thread, and you will see it over and over again. By the end of this book you will probably be saying to yourself (and to me)… ENOUGH ALREADY!

The strand that runs through all of this is that no matter how much information you have; what experts you have consulted with; how educated you may be; how much money you might have spent; how good your school is or how comprehensive a plan you think you have, in the end, both you and your child will not feel like a success, or feel that progress has been made, unless you follow these 3 simple guidelines:

- **CONSISTENCY;**
- **CARING; and**
- **FIRMNESS**.

The Old Way of Educating our Child has Changed

In a perfect world we would feel comfortable knowing that we, and our child, (who may have Attention Deficit and Hyperactive Disorder, a Learning Disability, Dyslexia, Obsessive Compulsive Disorder, or any of the other labels we may have attached to the unique personalities of our child) would have access to programs and personnel which would assist in the care and teaching of our child, and help to guide us through our challenging times. But during the past several years, due to declining funding, we can no longer make this assumption and it leaves us in a state of confusion, frustration and anger over how we are left to deal with this situation.

Part of the answer is that, as parents, we must now take on a greater degree of involvement in the management of our child's educational, social and behavioral needs. It is now time for us to recognize and take responsibility for creating significant academic and social growth for our children, both at home and in the educational system.

We have entered into a new time... a time where "the old way" of educating our children has changed.

We must reassess and develop a strategy on how we as parents are going to react to these changes in order to provide the best academic and social environment for our children in the coming years.

The "New Age" for parents and educators really can be seen as a "throw back" to past generations. Our role is to re-teach our children the values of: self-discipline, courage, compassion and responsibility within an environment that includes large classrooms, under trained personnel, impatience within the system, and a mentality that the best way to deal with a special needs child is to use a "quick fix", (which include medication, which we will talk about in a later chapter).

We must empower ourselves. That is, as the ultimate role model, we must take command of the fact that we are the parent, teacher, advisor and advocate for our child. It is our responsibility to know how to assess the problems that may exist within the home and at school, as well as knowing our child's academic strengths and weaknesses.

We need to look at our parenting style and see if it fits the needs of our child, because simply modeling the way in which we were taught and raised may not be the best method for this particular child. We need to look at our schedule and our child's schedule to determine how we can spend more quality guidance and playtime with them. Teaching them the importance of communication and relationship is paramount.

Whatever plan we create, we must ensure that success is guaranteed, for this will set the groundwork to develop and support self-esteem, responsibility and decision making skills for the entire family.

As parents we are "partners with our schools". This implies a number of responsibilities like expanding our contact and communication with the educators of our child, asking the appropriate and relative questions and establishing individualized programs that will meet the unique needs of our child.

So what does this all mean? Well, it means that

now YOU are the leader of your individual community. You are the principal role model. You are the motivator and the creator of positive energy. You are the one who by being CONSISTENT, FIRM and CARING teaches consistency, responsibility and strength of will. You are your child's partner and in this time of change you have the opportunity to make every difference.

The State of our Public System

Our politicians report to us on a regular basis as to the state of our Country, and as business people we constantly assess how we are doing and then make the necessary adjustments in order to meet our expectations of levels of achievement. We can, and should, follow the same process when dealing with the education of our child.

As parents, if you have not already realized it, it is important to be aware that our school systems have been undergoing some drastic changes for some years now. These changes in turn have had a marked effect on the type and quality of services that your child is receiving.

The fact is that during the last seven years, at the Federal and Local governmental level, we have cut several billion dollars from our education budgets. The result being, drastic cuts in special education personnel and programming.

There are about seven million children in North America, or some 12 percent, which were classified as requiring special educational services in 1998 (the last year for which data was available). The significant reduction in dollars directed to the care and education of your special needs child has resulted in making it harder to find, and keep, certified special education teachers. The paperwork and red tape leave these educators feeling swamped. To add insult to injury, with the introduction of "inclusion" (wherever possible, the special needs child is integrated into the population of a regular classroom), teachers have been made to feel overwhelmed by their inability to meet the demands of adequately teaching and providing the individual care which these children require.

For many parents and educators, as they are watching these children fall by the wayside, the most critical issue is the need to lobby for increased services and funding. Without a change in these practices special education funds will continue to be diverted to support more traditional forms of educational programming.

The district levels are faced with the task of how best to spend their dollars. They are in the precarious position of managing their teachers, parents and children with these dollars. It could be likened to a ship that has been torpedoed a number of times with water leaking in from all sides.

The schools are faced with larger class sizes, a population with more divergent needs, inadequate availability of curriculum supplies and dwindling special education services and after school programs. One of the results being an increase in the dropout rate and the other being a lack of resources to properly support the educational requirements of our special needs child.

These teachers are left with a greater degree of responsibility and fewer tools to work with. Large class sizes and inclusion, with minimal available support staff, help to create the conundrum. Teachers are not fully trained to deal with the various aspects of these special needs and literally cannot cope with the changing demands of their job. Needless to say it has played a role in creating the poor morale currently affecting our entire educational system.

It can be clearly seen that our children are the victims of an educational system that has been ravaged by declining funding. Articles have been written talking about the effect this has had on the motivation of high school students. They have lost their focus, do not wish to attend classes, and have lost their desire to work for higher degrees of excellence. Our younger children are caught up in the bureaucracy of a system that is failing to adequately support them. They are made to feel like failures at every turn.

As an educator and family counselor, I am party to the experiences that families are having with their schools. I am hearing first hand, the frustration and confusion of the parent who searches for a resolution to these declining resources without seeing any effective results for their efforts.

Self-Reflection – A Necessary Part

THERE IS NO MAGIC, Is about self-reflection and looking at the entire picture in order to effect necessary change within your family. Through this experience you will begin to see your role and responsibility to your child in a different way. You will see that it is not about the feelings of fear, anger, denial or frustration. Nor is it about the feeling of being sorry for yourself or in being the victim..., "What did I do to deserve this fate"? But it is about being open to the possibility that you can make a wonderful contribution to your child, and your child to you. That you have the opportunity to be a teacher, guide and advocate to your child. You have the opportunity to teach about compassion, understanding and responsibility to another human being by being that compassionate, understanding and loving human yourself.

So let us see all of these obstructions and problems as a challenge that allow us to teach another, who we really are. We are ready to teach our children to feel better about themselves, safer and more confident. We are ready to experience a higher degree of success as parents. We are really ready to bridge the gap and create a more harmonious family experience.

THEN WE CAN SAY THAT WE HAVE DONE THE JOB THAT WE CAME HERE TO DO…

TO TEACH, AND BE TAUGHT BY, OUR CHILDREN!

In writing this introduction, I have tried over and over again to visualize what it would look like. I was inspired by a movie called "I am Sam". This amazing piece of art depicts much of what it is truly about to be a parent, what it is to be a family.

"I am Sam" has so much inspired me. It is a movie about a single parent father who happens to have a genetic disability. He has an IQ of about 70 and functions on the general level of a seven-year-old child. The story begins as he was seeing and experiencing the joy of his daughter being born. The mother left right after birth and he was left to his own limited devices to bring up this child, and so he did. He did it with the innocence, honesty, purity and compassion of who "he" was. He did it the only way he knew how, and that was to share his unconditional love, acceptance and respect with this new being. As his daughter moved from birth to six, the time they spent together was filled with sharing and mutual learning. She had developed as a perfectly "normal", quite bright and very perceptive child, but at some point she began to understand that her father was "different" from other adults. What a wonderful gift she gave her father as she mirrored back to him the sense of love, loyalty and the passion, which he felt and had raised her by. It didn't take a genius to teach these basic life skills to a child.

The lesson portrayed here was that nothing could break the bond that they had for one another. This mutual respect had allowed for them to share, teach, and learn from one another. This handicapped parent and his daughter were teachers to each other and set new boundaries for society to learn from. For not only did they show us how exceptionally well they related to each other, but also how the community around them saw them as dysfunctional and in need of intervention, when clearly, in many ways, it was not the case. They became role models for others to see that bonds of trust, compassion and love between parents and children, no matter what the challenge, can never be broken.

If we can take a message like the one portrayed here, and allow it to help us realize the strength that comes with unity and unconditional love, love that does not allow any room for judgement or expectations; a love that provides a relationship which can be likened to a wave we see on the water, "flawless and ever present";

love which is not affected by guilt or shame, then we truly can overcome any and all obstacles that are placed before us, including that of being given the gift of raising a special needs child.

And through it all I invite you to always keep one thing in mind, and that is that...

THERE IS NO MAGIC.

CHAPTER 1

How we Define an Exceptional Child

How do we define "Exceptional Child"?

Exceptional children are those who, because of certain atypical characteristics, have been identified by professionally qualified personnel as requiring special education, planning or services, which differ from the status quo. Exceptional children are identified on the basis of their physical health, a sensory handicap, an emotional handicap, behavioral problem or by an observable exceptionality in mental ability. There are some children who, when accurately diagnosed, show more than one type of exceptionality.

For years we have been moving towards non-categorical descriptions to define an exceptional child. These children are now being defined by their special educational needs, rather than by a specific handicapping condition. The trend is towards looking at the child in terms of what educational needs might be required, as opposed to labeling the child as having any specific handicap.

The following comprehensively describes various exceptionalities, and gives descriptions of some of the characteristics that go along with them.

Attention Deficit & Hyperactive Disorders ("ADHD")

Attention Deficit Disorders are diagnosed into two categories: ADHD and ADD (without the hyperactive component). ADHD is a neurobiological disorder. Typically, children with ADHD have developmentally inappropriate behavior, including poor attention skills, impulsivity, difficulty sitting still, high energy, always moving around, disorganization and have difficulty in focusing, whereas ADD involves poorly focused attention, disorganization, a slow thinking process and decreased fine motor speed.

ADHD impacts on 4 essential functions:

1.   Operation of Working Memory

- Children have difficulty holding information in their mind while working on a task (short-term memory loss).

- This short-term memory is crucial to doing things on a timely basis and prevents them from being goal directed, or being capable of thinking ahead, plan or having adequate hindsight.

- Internalization of self-directed speech.

- Speaking out-loud to themselves.

2.   Controlling emotions, motivation

- These controls help to achieve goals, delay gratification and behave in socially acceptable ways. The ADHD child is without these skill sets.

3.   Reconstitution

- These skills help with discernment and decision-making.

- Breaking down of observed behaviors.

- Flexibility and creativity.

ADHD Characteristics

ADHD is diagnosed according to certain characteristics described in the Diagnostic Statistical Manual of Mental Disorders ("DSM-IV").

A child with ADHD is often described as having a short attention span; as being distractible; as having developmentally inappropriate impulse control and motor activity; as well as being disorganized, and as having slow cognitive processing and decreased fine motor speed.

- The child will have difficulty with focusing (picking something on which to pay attention), sustaining focus (paying attention for as long as needed) and shifting focus (moving attention from one thing to another).

- According to the DSM-1V, some symptoms of inattention include failure to give close attention to details and making careless mistakes in schoolwork or other activities.

- Often has difficulty sustaining attention in tasks or play activities.

- Often appears to not be listening when spoken to directly.

- Often has difficulty following through on instructions, does not finish schoolwork, chores or responsibilities due to inappropriate behavior or their failure to understand instructions.

- Often has difficulty organizing tasks and activities.

- Often avoids, dislikes, or is reluctant to engage in tasks that require sustained mental effort.

- Often loses things, which are necessary for undertaking tasks or activities (e.g., toys, school assignments, pencils, books).

- Is often easily distracted by outside stimuli like noises and movement.

- Is often forgetful in daily activities.

- Some symptoms of hyperactivity include: fidgeting with hands or feet or squirming in seat; not staying put in situations when remaining still is required; often runs about or climbs excessively; has difficulty playing or engaging in leisure activities quietly; is "on the go" or acts as if "driven by a motor"; excessive talking.

- Impulsiveness with ADHD appears when children act before thinking. Symptoms include: blurting out answers before questions have been completed; difficulty awaiting their turn; and interrupting or intruding on others rather than exhibiting patience.

What Should a Thorough Evaluation for ADHD Include

Do you know an ADHD child when you see one? Given the frequency with which children are diagnosed with ADHD, it is an increasingly likely diagnosis, when a child begins to exhibit inattention, impulsiveness, and/or hyperactivity.

During this period of decreased funding to our school and reduction of special needs programming and the inclusion of special needs children into the mainstream classroom, there seems to be a much higher incidence of ADHD diagnosis.

It becomes ever so more important that parents educate themselves and be aware of signs and symptoms that may indicate the presence of a problem other than, or in addition to ADHD. The next step would be to know the process for evaluation with the goal being the development of an educational and social plan designed to meet the individual needs of your child.

There are four major categories of causes for symptoms that may be mistaken for ADHD:

Medical - The list of illnesses that have been overlooked or misdiagnosed in the presence of ADHD symptoms is long. Some of the conditions included are migraine headaches, traumatic brain injury, Asperger's Syndrome, learning disabilities and substance abuse disorders.

Social - A child may often react to a new situation in his/her school, family or peer group with different moods or behaviors such as inattention, anxiety, low energy, high energy, short attention span, lack of focusing. Focusing on the child's problems, without intervening to help the child deal with the cause or stress will not deal with the fundamental problem.

Psychological - Psychological conditions that can cause ADHD like symptoms include oppositional defiance disorder, mood disorders, and childhood depression. Medications and/or therapy may be included in the appropriate treatments for these conditions.

Finally, ADHD is often only one part of the picture. Treatment of the child's other conditions as well are crucial for success to be attained. Such treatments are unlikely unless there has been a thorough Psychological and Psychiatric evaluation with identification and recommendations of these associated conditions.

Diagnoses of ADHD

Given the ease with which a number of conditions or circumstances can "look like" ADHD, any child being diagnosed and treated for ADHD deserves a thorough evaluation. Evaluations should consist of a number of components, including:

1. A routine physical examination done by a pediatrician or family physician.

2. A thorough and detailed medical and family history.

3. A review of school records for any notable regarding grades or behavior.

4. Reports from the child on his/her perceptions of the learning environment and home situation.

5.	Reports from family members and current teachers about behavior, activity level and mood.

6.	Educational screening to look for learning difficulties and for academic strengths and weaknesses.

7.	A clinical psychiatric evaluation to look for the presence of other psychological issues that may be inhibiting the child's performance.

8.	A neurological screening.

9.	Laboratory testing, including basic blood chemistries and a complete blood count.

While a good pediatric examination will detect most serious problems, it is important to watch for signs of a medical problem. Abrupt weight gain or loss, marked changes in sleep patterns, marked fatigue, lack of interest in fun activities, or an increased need for rest or sleep, can all be signs of medical problems that can at times mimic ADHD.

Learning Disabled

Learning Disabled individuals are those who exhibit a disorder in one or more of the basic psychological processes involved in understanding or using spoken or written language. These disorders may be manifested in difficulties with listening, thinking, talking, reading, spelling or mathematics. They include conditions that have been referred to as perceptual handicaps, brain injury, dyslexia, aphasia and dysgraphia.

The following are the common terms used in describing the learning disabled:

1. ***Dyscalculia*** A severe difficulty in understanding or using mathematical symbols and concepts. Children who have Dyscalculia may have problems performing even the simplest mathematical calculations.

2. ***Dysgraphia*** A severe difficulty in producing handwriting that is legible and written at an age-appropriate level.

3. ***Dyslexia*** Difficulty in using and understanding language. Reading disabilities affect 2 to 8 percent of elementary school children.

Consider, that to read you must simultaneously:

- Focus attention on printed words and control eye movements across the page;

- Recognize the sounds associated with letters;

- Understand words and grammar;

- Build ideas and images;

- Compare new ideas to what you already know; and

- Storing of ideas into memory.

Scientists have found that a significant number of people with Dyslexia share an inability to distinguish or separate the sounds in spoken words.

Problems may occur in the areas of listening, reading, spelling and/or writing. Despite these difficulties persons with Dyslexia can be creative and talented. They often excel in the visual arts, drama, sports and mechanics.

4.   ***Dysnomia*** A marked difficulty in remembering names or recalling appropriate words when having a discussion. The problem may be particularly prominent if the person is asked to answer a question to which he/she must find an immediate answer.

5.   ***Non-verbal Learning Disorder (NLD)*** This is a neurological syndrome affecting the right hemisphere of the brain. People with NLD usually have outstanding verbal abilities and do well in subjects requiring reading, writing and speaking skills. They learn best through listening and speaking. NLD might be considered the exact opposite of Dyslexia.

The three major non-verbal skills affected are:

•   Motor co-ordination - There could be severe balance problems and difficulty with fine motor function, such as handwriting skills.

- Visual-spatial organization – There is a lack of understanding of spatial relations such as difficulty following directions.

- Social skills - This deficit could lead to an inability to use and understand non-verbal communications such as eye contact or body language. It tends to show up when making transitions to new things or having poor social judgement, which affects their interactions with others.

6. *Memory Disabilities*   People with memory disabilities may have difficulty with short-term memory. They have trouble remembering names, numbers, facts and even what may have happened a few minutes prior.   This presents problems in academic studies, preparing for tests, interviews or just plain old everyday social interactions.

7. *Auditory Perceptual Problem*
    Are individuals who have trouble taking information in through the sense of hearing and/or processing information that is heard. People with this problem frequently do not hear with accuracy. A discrimination error can change the meaning of the entire sentence. For example one might hear "I waited for the taxi", instead of " I went over to the taxi". People with auditory handicaps may not hear the entire word, for example they may

hear "formed", instead of "performed". Some auditory handicaps are:

- Auditory discrimination - Difficulty telling the difference between similar sounds such as "th" and "f" or "m" and "n".

- Auditory figure-ground - Difficulty hearing sounds over background noises: e.g., being able to listen to someone else while the television is on or being unable to hear the telephone ring while the radio is on.

- Auditory sequencing - Difficulty hearing sounds in the correct order. For example, they may hear "nine-four" instead of "four-nine", or "treats" instead of "street".

8. ***Visual perception Disabilities*** Difficulty in processing and/or interpretation of visual information. The types of visual perception difficulties are:

- Visual figure-ground – This is a difficulty in distinguishing between a specific image and a competing background. For example finding someone in a crowd, finding an object on a crowded desk, picking out a word in the middle of a sentence. People with this disability have difficulty spotting things.

- Visual sequencing - This is a difficulty in seeing things in the right order. A person with this disability sees words, letters or numbers in reverse. This causes significant difficulties with reading and writing.

- Visual discrimination – This is a difficulty in seeing differences between two similar objects. Someone with this problem cannot distinguish between a "v" and "u" or "e" and "c". They may also have trouble telling the difference between two shades of a color.

- Depth perception - This is a difficulty in perceiving distances. A person with this disability has trouble telling how far or near an object is. For example one may have difficulty in judging the distance from one step to another, or stepping off of a curb or misjudging the corner of a table.

9. **Cognitive Disorganization** Difficulty thinking in an orderly, logical way. People often jump to conclusions and have difficulty in planning tasks.

10. **Crossing the Midline** The individual has trouble moving one's legs or arms across the center of the body. This could include difficulty writing across a page, walking a straight line, sweeping a floor or catching a ball.

11. **Intersensory** Trouble using two senses at once, for example being able to feel someone touch you while you

are on the telephone or being able to listen to conversation while driving.

12.   *Motor Disability*

- Perceptual motor - Difficulty performing a task requiring coordination of what one sees and their hands. This is due to the fact that the brain is not processing the information properly. It may result in clumsiness, difficulty participating in sports or writing.

- Visual motor - Trouble seeing something and then doing it, learning to dance while watching a teacher, copying something off of the blackboard, playing catch. Here again the brain is not giving off the correct signals.

- Auditory motor - Trouble hearing something then doing it. Following verbal directions in sequence, dancing, taking notes[7].

13.   *Obsessive Compulsive Disorder*. Is an anxiety disorder characterized by uncontrollable intrusive thoughts or actions? Symptoms frequently cause considerable distress and interference with daily social or work activities. There may be a major preoccupation with the smallest of details in daily life. Obsessive ideas may be about dirt, disease, germs, quality of work, or real/imagined trauma. People may recognize their obsessive thoughts, but are unable to stop them. These

obsessive thoughts frequently lead to compulsive behaviors such as washing hands, cleaning things up, erasing, toe tapping, counting or saying words repeatedly.

14. ***Orthopedically Impaired*** There is a diverse range of disabilities in this category including: Cerebral Palsy, Spina Bifida, amputations, Muscular Dystrophy or any serious accident which causes a severe impairment to one's legs. Other health impairments include convulsive disorders, Cystic Fibrosis, heart disease, sickle cell, Hemophilia, Asthma, Rheumatic Fever, cancer, or any other chronic or acute health problem that limits vitality or alertness and adversely affects the students educational development.

15. ***Tourette Syndrome*** Tourette syndrome is a tic disorder. Tics are any sudden, rapid, recurrent, involuntary action or vocalization. Tourette sufferers display both motor and vocal tics.

Based on the DSM-IV, the criteria for Tourette syndrome are:

• Both multiple motor and one or more vocal tics which have been present at some time during the illness although not necessarily concurrently.

- The tics occur many times a day, usually in bouts, nearly everyday or intermittently throughout a period of more than one year and during this period there was never a tic free period of more than three consecutive months.

- The disturbance causes marked distress or significant impairment in social, occupational or other important areas of functioning.

- The onset is before age 18 years.

- The disturbance is not due to the direct physiological effects of a substance (e.g., stimulants or a general medical condition such as Huntington's disease or post viral encephalitis).

Blindness

A person is considered legally blind when the best corrected visual acuity is 20/200, or the person's visual field is 20 degrees or less. It is not true that all blind people have no sight; in fact, most blind persons do have some remaining vision. A person may be considered blind when he/she can no longer drive safely, has difficulty reading a newspaper, or cannot see objects in their peripheral vision.

One is blind to the extent that they must devise alternative techniques to do those things, which they would do with sight if they had normal vision. The government has established that a blind person has the following difficulties:

- Inability to see or to pass the eyesight test for a standard driving permit even with the use of corrective lenses.

- Inability to recognize by sight a known person across a moderately sized room.

- Total inability to recognize colors, (color blindness).

- Inability to read ordinary newsprint even with the use of corrective lenses.

- Inability to walk safely without bumping into things.

Communication Disordered

Individuals with communication disorders are those who exhibit impairments in speech and/or language (including impaired articulation, stuttering, voice impairment and a receptive or expressive verbal language disorder).

Deafness

Those who are unable to hear well enough to be confident to rely on what they are hearing and be able to use it as a means of communication or processing information.

Common causes of hearing loss are:

- Childhood illness (Spinal Meningitis and Rubella, German Measles.

- Pregnancy-related illnesses (such as rubella, German Measles or drug/alcohol abuse).

- Injury (a severe blow to the head can cause damage to the eardrum and initiate hearing loss).

- Excessive or prolonged exposure to noise.

- Heredity factors.

- The effects of aging.

Deaf-Blind

Deaf-blind individuals are those who have been diagnosed as having both hearing and visual impairments, the combination of which causes severe communication and other developmental and educational problems.

Developmentally Disabled

The term "developmental disabilities" refers to a disability attributable to mental retardation, cerebral palsy, epilepsy, or other neurological conditions of an individual, found to be closely related to mental retardation or to require treatment similar to that required for mentally retarded individuals. In addition, the developmentally disabled are evidenced by a severe, chronic disability which:

- Is attributable to a mental or physical impairment, or a combination of mental and physical impairments.

- Is manifested before the age of 22.

- Is likely to continue indefinitely.

- Reflects a need for a combination, and sequence, of special interdisciplinary or generic care, treatment or other services, which are lifelong, or extended in duration.

- Results in substantial functional limitations in any three or more of the following areas of life functioning:

  - Self-care;

  - Understanding and the use of Language;

  - Mobility;

  - Self-direction in setting goals and undertaking activities to accomplish these goals; and

  - Living independently.

Behavior Disordered

A condition in which the individual exhibits one or more of the following characteristics over a long period of time and to a marked degree:

- An inability to learn which cannot be explained by intellectual, sensory or physical health factors.

- An inability to build or maintain satisfactory interpersonal relationships with peers and teachers.

- Inappropriate behavior or feelings under normal circumstances.

- Pervasive mood of unhappiness or depression.

- At times being unable to control one's anger and acting out in a manner that may be self-destructive or destructive to those around.

- A difficulty in following rules and adapting to limits.

Health Impaired

Health impaired individuals are those whose educational progress is restricted because of limited strength and vitality or alertness due to chronic health problems such as a heart condition, tuberculosis, rheumatic fever, nephritis, asthma, sickle cell anemia, hemophilia, epilepsy, lead poisoning, leukemia, diabetes, cancer or other illness.

Special Needs Of The "Gifted And Talented" Child

Although most of us would opt for this to be our choice of exceptionality, if we had to have one, *Gifted and Talented* children are faced with their own set of challenges. These children have traits and characteristics, which set them aside from "mainstream" children. Because these individuals have outstanding abilities in one or more domains, i.e., intellectual, artistic or sensory-motor, and because educators may not recognize these abilities, or may not have the available resources, they are often not taught at their capacity of understanding. It is estimated that over 15% of the student population may be identified as "gifted" or "talented". We must detect this uniqueness about them at the first available opportunity and provide them with the stimuli to keep them from the boredom and drudgery of functioning at a level far below their capacity. These children need, and most definitely demand, more challenging material. More challenging, certainly than that of their age group and in some cases, more challenging than that of those older generations. These can be children who become our geniuses, our "Einsteins".

Evaluation for the Exceptional Child

If your child is experiencing academic, behavioral or social problems, you can consult with the Educational Support team from your school. As a parent you can make the referral for an educational and psychological assessment. The team is usually made up of an administrator, classroom teacher, a special education teacher and school psychologist. A comprehensive individual evaluation needs to be conducted before the child can receive any special services.

The results of the assessment should specifically identify both the academic and social strengths and weaknesses of the child. Recommendations and strategies should follow.

Once the evaluation is completed the results are integrated with family history, medical history, academic record and educational environment. The team then uses this information to make practical recommendations for home management, class placement, educational programming, intervention strategies and appropriate teaching strategies and materials. As a parent if you do not agree with the evaluation you have the choice of doing an independent evaluation by a qualified Educational Psychologist.

As part of a comprehensive assessment the following areas are looked at:

- Intelligence
- Language Functions
- Memory Functions
- Motor Functions
- Visual Processing
- Academic Functions
- Emotional Functioning
- Auditory Functioning

Intelligence

All students being evaluated for educational and/or emotional support must be administered an intelligence test done by a psychologist. The intelligence test looks at skills that are required to learn in school. This includes verbal comprehension and expression, vocabulary development, verbal and non-verbal reasoning, numerical reasoning, and problem solving ability, auditory and visual short-term memory and long-term memory, visual perception and visual motor coordination. During the testing the evaluator is noting the child's ability to attend and concentrate, what kind of motivation they have, flexibility, mood and organizational skills.

So the results become a predictor of academic and social achievement.

The most frequently used tests are:

1.   Wechsler Intelligence Scale for Children (WISC)

2.   Stanford-Binet Intelligence Scale

3.   Woodcock - Johnson Psycho-Educational Test

Language Functions

This part of the assessment looks at speech skills. Speech skills test for articulation, voice and fluency in our speech.   Language skills include grammar, vocabulary and auditory processing. It is broken down into "Expressive Language" which is the ability to express oneself verbally and "Receptive Language", which is the ability to understand the spoken word.

Memory Functions

This part of the assessment looks at "Auditory Memory" and "Visual Memory". Auditory Memory is the ability to remember information orally.   Auditory Sequential Memory is the ability to remember details as presented orally. It could be a number of sounds or syllables in a word or a series of words in a sentence.

Visual Memory is the ability to remember things presented visually. Visual Sequential Memory is the ability to remember details given visually in a specific order.

The third aspect here is the ability to remember things presented both visually and orally. This quite often is an area of difficulty for the ADHD or learning-disabled child.

Motor Functions

This part of the assessment looks at fine motor skills, demonstrated when using a pencil, buttoning a shirt or tying one's shoelaces. The evaluator is also looking at the speed with which the tasks are performed.

Auditory Processing

This assesses the child's ability to differentiate among sounds and words that are similar. More specifically it tests sound recognition, sound blending and spelling skills. It also looks at one's ability to filter out background noises. This is a common difficulty for children with learning difficulties or ADHD.

Visual Processing

This part of the assessment looks at the child's ability to process what is seen. It translates into being able to identify, shapes of letters, numbers, words, pictures or objects. It is also the ability to separate out an object from a background (e.g.: seeing a car positioned in front of a mountain). The evaluator is also looking at the speed with which the child processes the visual information.

Academic Functions

Reading- Basic reading skills include word attack and sequencing skills used to decode unfamiliar words. Reading comprehension, which is the ability to understand the meaning of the written language, and Reading rate, which is the speed with which the material is read with comprehension.

Written Expression - is the ability to express ideas in writing with appropriate vocabulary, spelling and grammar.

Mathematical Computation - is the ability to calculate and understand number concepts and their operations.

Emotional Functioning

This provides information with regard to the child's control and frustration levels. It looks at the child's feelings towards himself/herself, family, peers and school. This area determines if there are emotional conflicts which are inhibiting the learning and developmental abilities of the child.

As parents it is in your best interest to be prudent when an exceptionality is diagnosed for your child. In providing appropriate interventions and treatments for young people with exceptionalities, the importance of a thorough assessment cannot be overemphasized.

In Summary

Whatever the exceptionality may be, we know that there are many accompanying concerns by parents and a host of feelings that both the parent and child go through. The confusion, anger, doubt, fears and many questions continue to create quite a challenge for the family. It is important to stay focused and positive because these issues will not go away without being addressed.

What will help is to keep moving forward. Get the opinions and assessments from qualified professionals, but keep it in mind that when putting together your parenting plan, that all of the elements should be designed to meet the individual needs of both yourself and your child.

To have an exceptional child is quite a challenge in itself. You will find that the majority of the support available is for the child. But what about you and what your facing? It is imperative that you seek whatever support you may need to help you continue to move forward on a positive note. Build this support system into your daily ritual. Check in with yourself often to see just where you are, where your stress levels are. We must be 100 percent and then some, before we can give of ourselves effectively. If we are not, we will find ourselves in a state of depletion and no good for ourselves, let alone anyone else. Take good care of you!

Some consideration may be given to:

- Finding parent groups with children of similar conditions;

- Choosing activities that offer fun and relaxation for both you and your child; and

- Being involved with organizations that will allow you to keep up with research and information specific to your situation.

Remember we all have exceptionalities in one form or another. The key is to create a positive attitude and successes based on our inherent strengths.

An Excerpt from the Author–"See Spot"

As individuals and parents we realize that there are many stages of development as we move through life. It has been my experience that if we deal with our challenges, with our sense of humor we can minimize the drama around our problems. So to add a little levity here I have written a piece, which is called, "See Spot."

This precedes the next chapter on how we may better understand ourselves and how this may help us in knowing our children.

····· See Spot ·····

Imagine all of the opportunities that we have during our lifetime. We are born with the gifts of innocence, curiosity, compassion, understanding, discernment, love and the knowing of the universal truths.

There are many "SPOTS" that make up one lifetime. Possibly but not probably the first is our "BIRTH SPOT". This sets the stage for us to play our part in the further development of the community.

During this SPOTLESS journey we learn things such as joy, fear, satisfaction, greed, fulfillment, sadness, guilt, joy, failure, joy, confusion and joy.

It is almost as if it is up to us to balance the stuff that we came into this SPOT with, what we learn when we are confronted with the different SPOTS that happen in our life.

After our BIRTH SPOT we mosey along through our CHILDLIKE SPOTS. These are interesting because we get to practice and show off all of the gifts that we started with. Because there is so much purity in this SPOT life is full of cooing, smiling funny faces, touching and dancing. Essentially lots and lots of partying and in return this SPOT is full of love. It is like a getting to know you SPOT. Everybody is wooing each other.

Although our worlds are still filled with much curiosity and play, as we continue to meander through our CHILDHOOD SPOTS we begin to sense different rhythms. Often these rhythms place a little furrow in our brow. At first we don't understand these new rules and expectations and for sure we have **BIG** problems with this new word that we keep on running into called... **NO**. Boy what a SPOT to be in here. We are not quite sure what to do. On one hand, we want to please those around us and, on the other we know that these new restrictions are going against those things that we know to be right.

The world automatically becomes darker and our bodies take on a more foreboding feeling. In this SPOT we may become more hesitant, confused, defiant, angry, withdrawn or whatever else. Of course we do not know these words... this is just what our bodies are telling us in this SPOT we're in. But of course we are not going to let a little thing like "NO" stop us, so we continue bopping along, hand in our pockets..., or not, with a whistle in our song and a swagger in our stride.

Along the road we run into a lot of young minds just like ours. Then, all at once there are SPOTS everywhere... spots called school, spots called friends, spots called teachers, and spots called principals. This big, old world is becoming one heck of a SPOT to be in. We are learning to make all of these decisions - on the SPOT. When we think we've finally figured out what spot we're in, we get to see those darn SPOTs change..., Yep, right before our eyes. Just when we seem to be getting comfortable again we grow these BIG RED SPOTS on our faces, our bodies start to change and though we don't understand why, we get the feeling that we are the only one in this SPOT on the planet and that everyone has to listen to us..., and they don't.

We begin searching, although what for, we do not know, but search we must and search we do. You know, at times, it doesn't feel so much like this is a very EXCITING SPOT to be in.

SEE SPOT RUN through this early opportunity to check in with its' origin and decide what to do with all of these new teachings they are being asked to learn. We get the opportunity to make decisions about our independence, about our home life, about new, vibrant, stimulating relationships between others and ourselves. WOW, is this not THE SPOT to be in or what? We get to examine our self-esteem and are actually able to watch it develop as we make decisions for ourselves and continue to learn about whom we are.

You think it is over..., not by a long SPOT!

The Awakening Spot

Because we have this wonderful opportunity to enlighten ourselves, we awaken and get to experience the journey by seeing the spots as we come to them. We get to choose what to do as we are confronted with each and every one of these SPOTS and just in case you hadn't noticed, I need to tell you, these spots are getting **BIGGER** and **BIGGER** and **BIGGER** all the time now. As our responsibility grows so do these spots.

From here we rocket into a time filled with even greater responsibilities, huge challenges and opportunities to practice all of which we learned, from way back there at the BIRTHING SPOT, right up to this very moment. We have an opportunity to look at who we are and where we want to go next. We go to university, get jobs, make money, buy houses, get married (not necessarily in this order), have kids…, Uh oh, have we come to the KIDS SPOT?

Now it becomes our turn. We are starting the CIRCULAR SPOT all over again, and tell the truth does this mirror not bring up every single spot imaginable? ;o)

During this time we get to choose to:

- See SPOT run (it may be backwards or forwards)
- See SPOT walk
- See SPOT be motivated by denial, or guilt, or fear, or greed, or love, or joy, or compassion, or…!
- See SPOT surrender or not!

It is what we do when we get to experience all of these spots that governs the type of life that we will lead during this lifetime. Remember that we can never go back, even though we may try when faced with a spot that is not so pleasant.

I offer each of you four things to think about in any spot, at any age, in any time:

1. **Acknowledge** the way you're feeling.

2. Ask yourself, **"What is it teaching me about me"**?

3. Ask yourself, **"How does this provide an opportunity for me to grow?"**

4. Realize that **you have the choice to change anything**.

After All

The One Thing We All Have In Common Is That

We're All In This To Find Our

●●●●●●*~ SWEET SPOT ~*●●●●●●

CHAPTER 2

Understanding Ourselves
Knowing Our Child

Becoming a Parent

As a new parent, we right away go to a place of believing that we no longer have the same degree of freedom. We forget that this was our choice. That freedom comes with taking on responsibility with grace and dignity.

Yes, no surprise, parenting is a lot of work. There's diapers, disciplining, the worry, car pooling, the scrounging for dollars at times, but when we look deeper and see what we are being given in return, we realize that it is life's most fulfilling experience. Children bring closeness, continuity and a magnitude of learning experiences and personal growth to our lives.

Choosing to have a family can ground us in a way that deepens our understanding of our own life and our service to humanity.

If we, both as individuals and as couples, are committed to the development of our family, the arrival of a child will just act to expand our degree of love for each other. Relationships will always be deepened and broadened when a child is born. It is our children that facilitate new opportunities for the expansion in our relationship with each other and with the world we live in. By the giving and receiving of love with our children, what was once feared and thought of, as a sacrifice becomes a joy.

What Empowers us as Parents

What empowers us as parents? It is the ability for us to be aware. To observe and reflect about what works or what doesn't and our flexibility to change.

Parenting can be complex. It is not about being good or bad or making the right or wrong choices, but rather, to being open to consider the fact that how we are currently parenting might be tweaked by the inclusion of new and different methods.

There is more than one choice in any given situation. By learning to be aware of the decisions we make and their result on both our children and ourselves, we can make the necessary adjustments within those choices, which may work in a more productive, beneficial way.

To be a parent means to make mistakes and to make them with a sense of humor and laugh about them together with our child, learn from each other and enjoy the experience together. It is about supporting our child's visions and gifts and challenges and finding the way that works best for you, as well as them.

Consistency, Firmness, Love

We have established that there is definitely a need for being consistent, firm and loving when it comes to taking care of the social and emotional needs of the family. All too often we get bogged down in the negative results of what we see in the educational and support systems within our community. At times the disruption and chaos that we are feeling overwhelms us. We then ask ourselves, what did we do wrong? We feel guilt, shame, anger and frustration. Do these emotions help to empower us? .... I think not, so we must focus on being proactive and making informed decisions when we go about creating this "new" game plan for dealing with our child's emotional and educational needs.

The steps may look like this:

- Look at those issues, the ones that always end with the same question, "why is this happening again"? The intent here is to avoid repetition of the previous strategies, which proved ineffective.

- Set new goals and strategies that revolve around attaining the desired successful result.

- Implementation of these new strategies by being consistent with their use, and delivered in a firm but loving way.

- Be Consistent, Be Firm, Be Loving.

As part of the implementation of the plan we must believe in what we are about to do and be 100% committed to this new plan. This commitment is the foundation for its ultimate success. You must feel satisfied that your plan is one that addresses every one of your concerns and requirements, as well as the reality that you will take the necessary steps to follow it through until the end... wherever that may be.

A Case Study

I would like to share with you my observations of one family and their experience with "Guilt". Remember no matter how hard it may seem or how painful for you and your child a situation might be, being consistent with your expectations, firm in your decisions and carrying through with what you said would be the consequence will truly lead to exceptional growth.

Not too long ago, I was working with a family who had two teenage sons. The father traveled quite a bit and mom had a part time job. Their 17 year-old was diagnosed with Attention Deficit Disorder and for several years had been having difficulty at school. He was above average in intelligence and very personable. Although he was very verbal and witty, he was also poorly motivated. When I came on the scene, Mom and Dad didn't know what to do. Their son was being openly defiant, not attending classes on a regular basis and withdrawing from the family. He would not honor his curfew, he'd walk out of the house and sometimes not come back for two or three days at a time. It should also be noted both Mom and Dad had had ongoing difficulty with enforcing family rules.

We had several family meetings to discuss both his and the needs of the family. The son agreed that there were difficulties to look at. He agreed to receive counseling and to follow the limits that his parents set for him. All of these agreements were broken within several weeks. His defiant behavior never diminished.

In one of our family meetings, we talked about his need of being responsible for his choices and life decisions and that for as long as he was living with Mom and Dad that he would have to follow the house rules. He was told that if he walked out of the house one more time without permission, or if he did not follow curfew and stayed out all night, that he would no longer be welcome in their home. In Canada, at the age of 16, a child can quit school and leave home at their own discretion.

It didn't take longer than a week for him to test this agreement that he made with his parents. As a matter of fact, after staying out the previous night he came home and started to pack a bag saying that he was moving out. Mom of course was very upset. Any parent can see that "tough love" is an extremely difficult position to be in. She took a courageous stance and watched him as he left the house. Of course he knew that he was no longer welcome back until he made the choice of following the family's guidelines.

Well, for three heart wrenching days he lived at a friend's house and on the fourth day he called and asked to return home, agreeing to a contract that allowed for him to be responsible for his behavior both at home and at school. One year later he is still there. He is much happier and is doing remarkably better in school.

In this case, Mom and Dad honored themselves, listened and acted upon the truth at hand and took a firm and consistent stand. The results were clear, their son felt safer and more secure knowing that his parents had things under control, something he was looking for all along

Are We Mr. & Mrs. Fix-Its?

One of the problems that we have is that when we see our child in need or in pain, the first place we go to is to "fix it" for them. In order to teach responsibility and independence we have to fight this urge and allow our children to resolve the situation themselves. By trying to make things "all better" we are actually dis-empowering the child.

When we look at it, by trying to "fix it" we are attempting to make the job an easier one for the child. It is most important to know when to step in and when we should step away. Have enough trust in your youngster, that they are capable of making their own choices, of getting themselves out of their own jams and making their own decisions. Respect them for at least attempting the task. Step in only when their choice may have the potential for harm.

This act alone is a supreme learning opportunity for the child. It shows them that you respect and have faith in their judgment. You are empowering them and building their self-confidence. For you it is a chance to let go, and allow your child to find and use its own set of life skills.

When we bring home a newborn our first inclination when we hear our child cry is to assume that there is something wrong with their world and we find ourselves running into their room to give them comfort. Face it, at this age, under typical circumstances, the needs of this infant are to eat, sleep, develop, discover, play a little and receive your nurturing. They get fed and changed every three to four hours and they let you know when they are ready for this the only way they know how, by crying or whimpering. Their instinct tells them that if they let you know they are in need, you'll come to the rescue. They cry for attention, and if we give them attention every time they cry…, well what do you think? Will they learn self-reliance? Does that child really need our constant relentless nurturing? Or, have we taught them to be dependent on it and unable to manage some things for themselves?

I have a funny story that I tell people about my second child, my daughter Chelsea. She would cry constantly at night and her mother would immediately run into her room to comfort her. This became quite a game between them. Chelsea was enjoying this immensely and so her crying became more and more frequent, because each and every time she cried, there was the reward of coddling. By the time she turned five months of age, her crying had increased in intensity and she ended up in hysterical fits and throwing up. This happened on three different occasions. The fourth time this cycle of behavior started, I tied my wife down (not really!!!) and went into Chelsea's room. In a very firm and authoritative voice, I said.... "Now stop crying... and Chelsea, no more throwing up either". Astonishingly enough, she looked at me began, to smile, laid down in her crib and went to sleep. Never again did she attempt to gain attention in that way. I could not believe my eyes. I realized the power that we give our children over us, and more importantly, the power that we can give to them by encouraging them to do things for themselves. Our children yearn not to be controlled but to be made to feel that they have our confidence in them, that they are capable of making their own decisions.

Much of the acting out we witness from a child, is when our kids are not feeling safe for one reason or another. Not knowing how to express this emotion to us, they seek our attention, but in a negative way. If you really look at it we have done the same as adults... HAVEN"T WE! We have quit or changed jobs, left relationships or stopped communicating, all because we were in fear, or because we've felt threatened in the situation.

When it comes to our children, it would be safe to say that they are wise enough to be given the opportunity to fix their own stuff (unless there is cause for concern of physical harm). Allow them the space to find their own way, the chance to experience their own power and to find their own strengths and capabilities. Let them get to know who they really are.

Looking at the Whole Picture

When you look at effecting change within your parenting style, you need to be sure to look at the entire picture. For example, if you were looking to create more profit for your business, you would not just look at the market. You would review your personnel, your systems, and your products in order to come up with a corrective plan. Your family is no different. To effect change you must look at yourself and the role that you are playing and the effect that you have on the behavior of your child. When you come to terms with the fact that both you and your child are contributors to the situation, opening up to the possibility of creating a revised plan is that much easier.

In creating a shift in our attitude, it is a fact of human nature that our child will shift simply because of the change of attitude we reflect to them. To confirm this just look at what happens when a person walks confidently into a somber meeting room with a smile on their face and a bounce in their step. Most of the people in that room will gravitate to that person, simply, because they hold a brighter prospect for the meeting, then what they had previously thought possible. That one person, changed the energy of the meeting altogether. Think of yourself as that leader. With simple practice, it becomes a part of our everyday lives.

You will need to check in with yourselves, to see if you are READY to effect change; if you are READY to scrutinize yourselves; if you are REALLY READY to

"Walk your Talk". Without being ready to initiate change for positive growth we are stuck where we're at. We've found our barrier to success.

CHAPTER 3

Our Parenting Style

It is important to realize the style of parenting you are using and the impact that style is having on the social and emotional development of your child.

The Four Parenting Styles

There is considered to be four main styles of parenting: indulgent, authoritarian, authoritative and uninvolved. Each of these parenting styles reflects naturally learned patterns of parental values, practices and behaviors.

We'll briefly examine each style.

1. ***Indulgent parents*** - (may also be classified as "permissive" or "non-directive) are more responsive than they are demanding. They are non-traditional and lenient, do not require mature behavior, they allow considerable self-regulation and avoid confrontation.

2. ***Authoritarian Parents*** - are highly demanding and directive, but non-responsive. They are obedience and status oriented and expect their orders to be obeyed without explanation or questioning. These parents provide well-ordered and structured environments with clearly stated rules and limits. Authoritarian parents can be divided into two types: non-authoritarian-directive, who are directive, but not intrusive or autocratic in their use of power; and authoritarian-directive, who are highly intrusive and controlling with their demands.

---

3. ***Authoritative parents*** - can be both demanding and responsive. They monitor and impart clear standards for their child's behavior. They are assertive, but not intrusive and restrictive. Their disciplinary methods are supportive, rather than punitive. They want their children to be assertive as well as socially responsible, and self regulated as well as cooperative.

4. ***Uninvolved Parents*** - are low in both responsiveness and making demands. They are passive and may have difficulty accepting responsibility for their behavior in the full parenting of their child.

To clarify some differences between the Authoritarian and the Authoritative parenting styles, both Authoritarian and Authoritative parents place high demands on their children and expect their children to behave "appropriately" and obey parental rules. Authoritarian parents, however, also expect their children to accept their judgements, values and goals without questioning. In contrast, authoritative parents are more open to give and take with their children and make greater use of explanations. Thus, although authoritative and authoritarian parents are equally high in behavioral control, authoritative parents tend to be low in psychological control, while authoritarian parents tend to be high.

As I was researching parenting styles, a few very interesting facts stuck out:

• Parenting style has been found to predict the child's well being in the areas of social competence, academic performance, as well as, psychological development and problem behavior.

- It was observed that children and adolescents whose parents are consistently authoritative are more socially and psychologically competent than those whose parents are non-authoritative. It was found that the more responsive a parent is, the more socially and psychologically balanced the child is, while parental demands are associated with how the child may do academically and behaviorally.

- It was observed that children and adolescents from authoritarian families (high in demands, but low in responsiveness) tend to perform moderately well academically and be disinterested in their problem behavior. That they have poor social skills, lower self-esteem and higher levels of depression.

- It was observed that children and adolescents from indulgent homes (high in responsiveness, low in demands) are more likely to be involved in their behavior and perform less well in school. That they have a higher self-esteem, better social skills and lower levels of depression.

It's interesting to note here that children who have parents who exhibit an authoritative style of parenting exhibit lower levels of acting out (problem behavior), are better socially adjusted and do better academically.

Since there are several types of temperaments your child may have, your parenting style may be influenced by your child's personality characteristics. In the next section we will discuss these different temperaments and how you may best adjust your parenting style accordingly.

Are we ready to see our children as feeling better about themselves, safer and more confident? Are we ready to experience a higher degree of success as parents? Are we really ready to bridge the widening gap and create a more harmonious family unit? Are we ready to take what we know about ourselves and our children and to take a stand and follow through on the big "Three" keys to successful parenting?

The three keys to successful parenting are:

1.   **Be CONSISTENT**
2.   **Be FIRM**
3.   **Be LOVING**

In adapting this to our parenting style, we can empower our child to be the very best they can be!

Traits of Children

Earlier in this chapter, we were discussing different aspects of ways that we may be able to better understand our child. What follows is some excellent information as to the type of temperament that your child may have. It provides descriptions of each, and gives some suggestions as to how to adapt your parenting style and the optimum learning strategies for each temperament in the hope that it will assist you in making parental and educational decisions.

An infamous psychiatrist named Carl Jung did extensive research on the differences and temperaments of children in an effort to familiarize parents with their child's needs.

He classified four differences that exist:

1. Introversion vs. Extraversion

2. Sensation vs. Intuition

3. Thinking vs. Feeling

4. Judgment vs. Perception

We will look at these four temperaments as they present themselves in childhood and then they will be examined as to how they affect the teaching of, and learning ability of a child.

Extraversion vs. Introversion

An Observation: Does the child show hesitation in approaching a stranger, teacher, an event, or does the child approach a stranger, teacher or event with enthusiasm and without apparent reserve?

The introverted child is likely to hold back when faced with something or someone unfamiliar, while the extraverted child is more likely to approach the situation without hesitation. The introverted child tends to be shy, quiet and less intrusive than the extraverted child. The introverted child is apt to take their time about a decision and be slower to respond, seeming to absorb the information before communicating. Because of this the introverted child may appear to be less intellectually capable than he/she actually is. The introvert reserves from "public view" aspects of their temperament, which are in the process of developing. What is presented to the "public" are those qualities already developed. There are parts of their real selves, which is not available to their teachers, parents and friends. They are sometimes seen as a puzzle waiting to unfold. They may be judged as being "stubborn" or lack self-esteem because of their desire to hold back until they are surer of what they wish to present of themselves. It is the introverted child who is most often misunderstood and pressured to change. Their tendency to be retiring and shy, their slower development of social skills, their tendency to draw back when confronted by a more assertive person, their slowness to interact in the classroom and their need for privacy, are all behaviors, which parents and teachers may attempt to correct. In the process of doing this what they may be communicating to this child is that their natural ways are wrong. How often have you heard someone say to a shy child, "Is there anything wrong? You are being so quiet". Quite often this just causes the introverted child to become even more withdrawn. For some reason we as adults become uncomfortable, or maybe personally threatened when we encounter a being that operates more from within.

On the other hand, the extraverted child is usually better understood and relates well to others. They are at home in their social environment and tend to be responsive, expressive and enthusiastic. They more readily enter into group activities. They seem to adjust better to changes in their lives and tolerate negative interactions better than the introverted child does. They tend to approach new situations quickly, to verbalize and act quickly. They exhibit a certainty in making decisions giving the impression of self-confidence. The extraverted child gets considerable more confirmation of their behavior and attitude, both from adults and other children, than does the introverted child. The consequence of this is that the extravert grows up with fewer doubts about themselves than their counterparts.

Sensation vs. Intuition

An Observation: Does the child daydream frequently and seem hungry for fantastic tales, even wanting them repeated over and over, or is the child more bent on action, getting involved in games and liking more factual stories?

According to research, the intuitive child is likely to ask for repetition of stories and likes stories that are fantasy related. The sensitive child likes the adventure story that is familiar and factual in nature. They want the story to make sense. They like stories with lots of detail. The sensitive child likes to engage themselves in playing games or activities that involve some form of action.

The intuitive child is likely to anticipate future events. Also, if a promise is made to the intuitive child, breaking that promise will result in major upset, where the sensitive child may take the change more in stride. The intuitive child may pose a behavior problem because they want to do "their own thing" or "be their own person". If they do not believe that someone is speaking the truth they will challenge their authority. They seem confident as to their intents and purposes as if they know what they are supposed to be doing. Adults may interpret this behavior as being defiant and this will often lead to discipline and conflict if one is not aware. In addition, because the intuitive child is often looking ahead, they may seem preoccupied and inattentive. Some of these qualities are associated with Attention Deficit and Hyperactive Disorder (ADHD). Both educators and parents need to be cautious because there are many cases where these children are identified and labeled with ADHD when such is not the case.

In addition, the intuitive child is passionate about their beliefs and if their trust is violated their feelings are likely to be hurt. They are honest and direct in their relationships with their peers and authority figures. They speak their mind, which they know to be the truth. As their parents and teachers, we often tend to think that these children are eccentric, live a life of their own or are troublemakers. This type of reaction to them creates a block in their creative processes and they can suffer considerable damage to their self-esteem.

Where the intuitive child may be daydreaming away the hours, the sensitive child is animated and very involved with their activities and relationships. The sensitive child responds well to details and loves to engage with those that are around him. Toys, for a sensitive child will retain their character. For example, a truck remains a truck to be used for hauling or storing, whereas for the intuitive child that same truck might be turned into a submarine or a monster that is able to fly.

Understanding these differences of both the intuitive child and the sensitive child can be vital to the academic and social development of both of these types of children. It is, however, the intuitive child who is most likely to be the one who seems, "odd".

Thinking vs. Feeling

An Observation: When asked to obey in a situation he does not quite understand, does the child tend to ask for reasons (thinking) or does the child tend to seek to please (feeling)?

The child who prefers the "thinking" way is likely to want an explanation for being asked to do something, while the child who chooses the "feeling" way will want some confirmation that he/she is pleasing the other person by his good deed. The feeling child is likely to be more sensitive to the feelings of others and is likely to want to do little things to help out and then be recognized for their accomplishments.

The feeling child is very sensitive to the emotional climate of their home and will react to the conflict and stress that they are feeling around them. On the other hand, the thinking child seems to find it easy to detach themselves from the disharmony happening around them. The thinking child may not want to be touched and may have difficulty in approaching a parent with affection while the feeling child responds easily with physical affection. The feeling child is likely to cry more easily than the thinking child is. Although the feeling child seems more vulnerable than does the thinking child to the approval or disapproval of a parent or teacher, this is usually a front or defensive reaction. The thinking child may seem to be indifferent and unresponsive, but inside they may be hurting or desiring just as much as the more expressive and open feeling child.

Perceiving vs. Judging

An Observation: Does the child seem to want things settled, decided and chosen or does he want to be surprised and have choices at all times?

The judging child, who seems to want things established and in order, probably has a tendency to be calculating and will more often than not weigh things before making decisions. The child who seems indifferent to authority figures, the perceiving child, may be the one who is reacting to his perceptions and his environment. It is the judging child who is likely to be ready and on time for appointments and tends to be neat and organized. The perceiving child may seem unconcerned about being on time, his room or desk may be a mess and they may have difficulty understanding why this type of behavior causes discomfort with teachers or parents.

The judging child is apt to be more of a leader within his peer group. The perceiving child often needs to be reminded to get dressed, to come to dinner, to do their homework or chores etc.

The judging child is more the more assertive one and initiates carrying out his/her daily routines. The judging child seems surer of themselves whereas the perceiving child may be more tentative and laid back.

The Four Temperaments in Children

In his research Jung broke up the temperaments of children into 4 categories. If you can identify your child it may help when making some decisions about your child's educational, social and emotional needs.

1. The Sensible Playful Temperament

This child is likely to be active. They love to eat and love to get "down and dirty". Leave them in the sandbox or backyard and they will find the nearest mud puddle to roll around in. This will undoubtedly lead to many reprimands, but as a parent we should be cautious about discouraging this behavior. After a while your child will be indifferent to the scolding. If you can treat it with lightness and humor you will see that you will be positively reinforcing this natural behavior in them. As they grow up they are more likely to approach their lives with a sense of being able to get right into the fray of things. Their rooms are likely to be a jumble of toys, clothes and assorted objects all in apparent disarray but absolutely perfect for the sensible playful child. I was witness to my brother displaying all of these characteristics, and today he has turned out to be quite the successful businessman.

You see? This child is really in a different zone from the one we operate in. Their attitude is "What difference does it make?" They would rather be off doing something that makes sense to them, like having fun.

Yet the sensible playful child can get really involved in an activity and stay there for hours at a time. He can spend hours with a musical instrument, only to lose interest the next day. Those who do not lose interest, and are adequately reinforced by their parents, become the outstanding performing artists, graphic artists and artists of all types. The sensible playful child needs movement and excitement and they thirst for competition.

You may be getting the picture that this is a very upbeat child and that they're really cheerful. They can bring fun and laughter into the home and classroom. They love to participate in activities, and they throw themselves wholeheartedly into instrumental play, musical performances, art activities and games. They may enjoy working with a variety of tools rather than the actual product they make. The more game-like the task the better it is for them. They love the ages of 3-6 because it is all fun and play and exploration, but as they move up through the grades and schoolwork becomes more a matter of following a specific curriculum and structure they often become disinterested. They do not like to prepare or "get ready" for anything and as the demand for concentration grows so does their restlessness. The result may be in the form of disruption of their class or acting out at home. They may be seen as very jittery, bored and not being able to focus well. At times they have been labeled as hyperactive or as having Attention Deficit Disorder. This brings on a panacea of negative behaviors, which include a low self-esteem and poor academic and social performances.

It is important that the sensible playful child be provided periods of quiet activities and training in relaxation such as Yoga, meditation, breathing and visualization exercises. They need space in which they can be active, but they also require their own private space. A learning carrel (desk with 3 sides to cut down on external stimuli) proves effective in facilitating the completion of their schoolwork.

The sensible playful child is likely to feel good about themselves and about those who have control over them if they are provided a great deal of room to move around. Lecture type presentations should be short, as should their reading activities. Quiet, learning activities are best mixed in with opportunities for the child to be active with some area of personal interest. Frequent change from individual work space, to a small group and then to large group activities will also help to better meet the sensible playful child's educational and social needs.

All of this is not to imply that they should not be given practice in concentration and limit setting. Of course they must also develop these abilities, but the first step to this development is to legitimize and recognize their natural preferences and their acute nature to be impulsive and to become easily frustrated.

Needless to say the sensible playful child can be a behavioral problem in school and at home. They do not respond well to our traditional ways of discipline. These are the children that are labeled as combative and defiant. Because they do not conform, these children learn to seek attention in very negative ways. An alternative to this is to recognize them for who they are and what they need in order to be successful.

Learning Style

These children require the freedom to get involved in physical activities, to learn in an environment of excitement where adventure and competition are part of the curriculum. Where sound, color and motions are plentiful. They love to get involved with musical instruments because this provides both hands-on activity and performing in front of groups.

They can be excellent team members if there is a competition. They gravitate towards music, drama, art, crafts, mechanics and construction. Anything that requires hands-on activity is a valuable learning tool for this child.

They are quite visual and kinesthetic in their learning styles and their curriculums should reflect and take advantage of these strengths.

If these kinds of activities are not provided, this child will most likely find other outlets, which may be disruptive. If they are forced to conform by being made to stand in line, waiting, conform to routines, wait for tomorrows, they will find this task less and less appealing. For the most part this child does far less in school then they could do had they been given sufficient incentive. This child will be a source of frustration to their parents, teachers and administrators, as these people will be trying to project their own desires and controls on them. The sensible playful child will have none of this. Their goals are to find out "who they are" and to be more in the moment.

2. The Sensible Judicious Temperament

The sensible judicious child is more sensitive and vulnerable to instabilities within their environment. They find security in knowing that their parents are unified and in control. If there are inconsistencies from one parent to the other regarding discipline and family policies this will create disharmony in this child's life. It should be noted that this statement is true for almost any child and is not just specific to the sensible judicious personality.

The sensible judicious child does best when their surroundings are familiar to them. Growing up with the same friends, in the same neighborhood and school system suits them best. They love to share with the extended family such as grandparents, uncles, aunts and cousins.

The sensible judicious child works best when there are established routines in place and they know what their responsibilities are. Their great source of pleasure is the approval they are given by adults as they go about their activities. As a matter of fact this reinforcement is vital to the development of their healthy self-esteem. They tend to adjust well to their school environment and daily routines. Since they flourish with structure, they thrive on activities such as workbook activities, repetition, reading aloud, spelling, factual aspects of social studies, science and history and any activity that requires drill. They pay attention to details and hold high standards of achievement for themselves and others. Good study habits are important and they learn best when kept on a schedule. They will try in earnest to please their teacher and will respond negatively to criticism. In college the sensible judicious child tends to focus on careers such as business, accounting, and teaching.

Learning Style

This child desires to belong within the family unit and later, when they enter school, to the classroom group. Responsibility, dependability, duty and service are words that are strongly associated with this child. This child thrives in the traditional classroom setting. They have a strong wish to please their teacher, basically because they mirror the teacher, this authority figure who sets structure and limits and where a sense of security is felt and developed. The values of the teacher are compatible with their own. Good study habits, doing homework as assigned and on time and following the assigned rules as directed are seen as worthwhile. They are conscientious and will attempt to do their best as long as they receive clear directions so that they know how to proceed with the activity.

The sensible judicious child acquires knowledge through searching for facts; through frequent review and traditional teaching materials (textbook and workbook) Programmed-learning materials are very effective tools for this child.

They are auditory and tactile, kinesthetic learners. That is to say, they learn best when they hear the information and write or say the response. They also do best with "hands-on" materials.

3. The Intuitive Thinking Temperament

The intuitive thinking child will tend to be a puzzle to those people around them. They may be classified as precocious; they tend talk at an early age and learn to read before going to elementary school. The intuitive thinking child is likely to ask a lot of "why" questions. "Why do the stars come out at night"? "Why does a bird fly"? "Why can't I fly like a bird"? "Why do I have to go to school when I can learn at home?" They are usually very independent children and are seen as nonconformists. They are extremely curious and learn best when given the freedom to explore. They will ask themselves, "What would happen if...", and then proceed to attempt to find the answer, sometimes resulting in getting themselves into trouble. For example, even though you may have told them a dozen times that the stove is hot and not to touch, they may have to see for themselves before believing you. Despite this, they tend to be obedient and compliant with issues that they are indifferent to. They tend not to be interested in coming into conflict with those around them. If punishment is administered as a result of their curiosity and investigations, they are apt to accept the consequences impersonally. They can be a frustration to their teachers and other authoritative figures because they stay somewhat detached in their reactions to discipline. The intuitive thinking child will quickly lose respect and ignore those who are not consistent and logical in their style of discipline. Sometimes as parents and teachers we say things or threaten with things that we cannot follow through on. This child learns quickly not to respond to these tactics.

Any physical punishment is deeply violating to the intuitive thinking child. His body is a source of endless exploration, as is his external environment. Because of this, they may over react to discipline in the physical sense. They see this as a violation to their mind, body and spirit.

They are seen as full of pride and dignified and they expect the same in others.

Parenting the intuitive thinking child mainly means HANDS OFF. The intuitive thinking child needs an abundance of opportunities to experiment, find out and get the answers. Attempting to shut off this experimental and exploration avenue will cause this child to act out, seek attention in negative ways and be disruptive.

Learning Style

The intuitive thinking child usually enjoys reading books and being read to. Their enjoyment in being read to is a function of their curiosity and through stories they encounter complexities and learning, which they cannot gain through their own reading. They can get deeply engrossed with a new toy or activity and play for hours at a time on their own. On the other hand they may lose interest in this toy just as fast and never go back to it again. Providing them with help and guidance when they ask for it, being patient with their endless questioning and allowing them the freedom and space they require in order to function within their world, will ultimately allow for them to grow up with a healthy and self-confident feeling about themselves.

They have a great hunger to learn and these desires are directly linked to their levels of ability and their self-confidence. They have difficulty is setting priorities and often need help with their organizational skills.

The intuitive thinking child is devastated by criticism of their skill and ability levels. They can be self-doubting and require vast amounts of positive reinforcement to develop a healthy sense of self. Sometimes, because of their early interest in the sciences, well meaning parents and teachers may expect too much from them, resulting in failure and withdrawal.

4. The Intuitive Feeling Temperament

At a very early age, these children display a gift for language. They are early talkers and love to partake in conversation. They can be very charming and love to play as they express their creativity through their talking. Because of this heightened degree of sociability they frequently will draw both their peers and adults around them. It is important to note that they are highly imaginative and that it is important for this quality to be reinforced. In addition, it is important to note that the intuitive feeling child may be hypersensitive emotionally to rejection and conflict, so they require reassurance that those around them are feeling good about themselves and in control.

The intuitive feeling child enjoys being read to, especially highly imaginative stories and may ask you to repeat the same story over again several times. They love to play with toys and can identify with their characters. It is common for this child to have and play with an imaginary friend. As a parent it is important to recognize and support your child and their character. This will help to develop self-esteem and will nurture their creativity, spirituality and ability to relate to others in later life. If the child's fantasies are rejected one can predict that the child will withdraw, become more fearful and less trusting of their world and the people in it.

Because the intuitive feeling child is quite sensitive they need to be gently guided through their successes and failures as they learn to stand up for themselves and fully walk with a sense of confidence through the complexities of life. A harsh and authoritative approach will again cause withdrawal and the seeking of attention in negative ways. A common form used is passive aggression.

Learning Style

Because of their outstanding linguistic abilities the intuitive feeling child will tend to do well academically. They are good readers with good comprehension skills. They are good communicators. They like to work in small groups and are very democratic and introspective by nature. They like to do activities that involve research, history and social studies. They use their perceptive skills to study people's attitudes and values. They can quickly discern in people what they like and dislike, how they behave, why they behave the way they do. All of this fascinates this child.

They are kinesthetic and visual learners. That is, they learn best when interaction occurs both visually and by touch in their world.

It would seem that they would choose careers that involve liberal arts, psychology and teaching.

We are all different. We want different things, have different goals and objectives, values, ethics, drives and impulses. Nothing is more obvious than this. We think differently, perceive, understand, and comprehend differently. As parents it is important to understand this about ourselves as well as our children. To explore new ways of looking at ourselves and the people in our lives. Not only are we what we have learned from our role models, but as unique individuals and spirits we all deserve the opportunity to be recognized individually and to be treated in the same manner. We deserve the opportunity to learn and explore our world as unique and gentle beings in order to walk through our life feeling good about who we are and ultimately to be exemplary contributors to our communities. It is our birthright to experience growth and recognize our responsibility to then pass it on to our loved ones.

Case Studies

The Dover Family

History

Recently an acquaintance dropped by my office to ask my advice about a problem he was having with his son. Charles was saying he was feeling frustrated because his twelve year old son Arlen was not listening to him. Although the boy was a good student, he hated to do homework. When inquiring about changes in his behavior during class time, no notable behavioral problems appeared to exist but Arlen was clearly being defiant at home.

We spent a few minutes talking and I suggested to him that I spend some time observing the family. He agreed and we set up a time where I could casually join the family for dinner one evening.

Prior to doing so, I met with Charles and his wife to get a more informed picture of what their concerns for Arlen were. Charles parenting style was authoritarian; he is highly demanding, directive and expects all orders to be obeyed without explanation. His wife is more lenient She is assertive, but not restrictive, and attempts to be more supportive than punitive.

They explained that Arlen, whose biological mother lives overseas, is torn as to whom to choose to live with. Neither parent wished to impose their will on him, but at the same time both were making their wishes very clear. He had already tested living within both households and found it difficult to make any kind of final decision on his own.

They continued by saying that although Arlen did not exhibit any outward anger, he chose to do it in passive ways. They were tired of the continuous discipline they needed to give.

They described Arlen as a good child but one that was lazy, unmotivated and not responsible.

I then spent some time interviewing Arlen. My initial observations were that he was very intelligent, and quite articulate. In addition I found him to be a warm, sensitive and quite compassionate person. He seemed ahead of his years in terms of emotional development.

My impressions were that this was a loving family who were very eager to find away to create a more harmonious flow to relating to one another.

Desired outcomes:

1.   For both Mom and Dad to be one with their expectations and delivery to Arlen.

2.   To be able to be consistent when setting limits for him and to be able to carry through with the consequences when setting limits.

3.   To do it in a loving and caring way without any loss of composure.

4.   To come to a decision as to what is in Arlen's best interest as to where he should reside.

My observations

I determined that parenting Arlen in a consistent but gentle way would be supportive for this very sensitive and gentle boy. This would help to eliminate the minor acting out that they were experiencing from him. It was important that all avenues of communication be open between everyone involved so that Arlen felt comfortable to discuss his confused emotions around his living situation. It was also very clear that this decision was too enormous and impactful for Arlen to make on his own. Making this decision was challenging his safety and security. In this case, my feeling was that all parenting authorities should take it upon themselves to come to an equitable solution to the situation and create as much of a harmonious resolve as possible.

Results

Initially there was a considerable power struggle between Charles and his new wife and Arlen's biological mother. Each felt confident in their ability to provide a nurturing and stable environment for raising their child.

Within Arlen's current home structure things took on a new light. Expectations and limits for Arlen's behavior were clearly set out. Consequences for inappropriate behaviors and rewards for achievement were determined.

At the beginning of this new management plan there was considerable upheaval. Arlen was not happy to be under such a strict regime and acted out.   All consequences were enforced and he was reminded at the same time that the alternative behavior had a far more enjoyable result. Within a short span of time desired behavior was the norm.

Arlen's Father and Stepmother made it clear to Arlen that he would not be the one making a decision as to where he lived. They had decided that if a compromise could not be made between the adults, a court would have to make the decision for them. The biological mother was informed and after lengthy discussions an amicable plan was decided on. Because it would mean a complete life-style change not only in the home but in schooling and culture as well if he were to move overseas, it was thought best for Arlen to remain in his father's home. Summers would be spent with Mom, getting to know her home, lifestyle and culture and if at a later date Arlen were to show interest in a move the situation would be reconsidered. Holidays were to be split between the two homes.

Note

At times without knowing it, our parenting style can place undue pressure on our child. This may cause acting out in ways, which we do not understand. In this case it was Arlen's sense of relief at the shift he sensed in parenting style which allowed him to relax and change his behavior.

Tommy's Story

History - *The following is a description of Tommy given by his parents.*

Tommy was a bright, sensitive and honorable 12 year-old child.

He was quite smart, always achieving A's and B's. Although he was good at reading, he never liked to sit down to do it and reading out loud was something we couldn't ever talk him into. It wasn't until the eighth grade that he began to display academic problems.

It was then that his general attitude changed. He became more somber and withdrawn. During puberty he developed some acne and became quite self-conscious about his appearance. Although he continued to get passing grades, it was evident that he was underachieving.

His behavior worsened through high school but even though he was underachieving, Tommy still managed to finish 11th grade with passing scores.

During his last year of high school, Tommy fell apart. There was a period of a month where he refused to go to school and just stayed at home. He only went to class about 70% of the time, he refused to do any of the work that was sent home for him and this resulted in him failing all of his classes.

Although he still played tennis, he seemed to have lost his competitive edge.

My Observations

After meeting with him the picture that I had of this child was that:

- He is not capable of communicating with his parents or perhaps even recognizing himself what the issues were.

- He repressed much of his feelings and anger.

- He felt lonely, unsupported as well as a deep sense of loss.

Evidently Mom and Dad had very high expectations that he had the ability to, and would become a professional tennis player. For many years he worked very hard to achieve this goal for them. Until the age of approximately 16 he did everything in his power to make it happen for them. Then, one day he realized what it would take to pursue this tennis career. He didn't believe in himself enough to think that he had what it took. At this point he gave up, got very angry and self-destructed. Tommy had poor self-esteem and lacked confidence. It seemed to him that his life was one-dimensional and even though he wanted to find a way back he didn't know how or where to start.

Desired Outcomes

Tommy and I had several private sessions together with the purpose of allowing him to unwind and just talk about what was going on in his life. We worked on creating a picture of who "Tommy" really was. This personable, sensitive sometimes-shy person who was gentle and functioned best when treated in a gentle way. As the pressures were released he became more comfortable with himself. He did not "hammer" himself so much with the thought that he wasn't good enough. Our focus was on allowing him to re-empower himself, and eventually he took complete control of the sessions.

Once he became comfortable with the self-discoveries he had made, we decided it was time to bring the whole family into the meetings to discuss some of the issues that helped to create some of these feelings of inadequacy he had had. Some of these things blocked his ability to perform and show everyone who he really was.

Results

The family meeting allowed Tommy to comfortably speak to his parents about some of the things that had taken place to create such high demands on what he was to do with his life. It also allowed him to see how open they were to listen to what he had to say and what he thought. They talked and responded with him in an open and honest manner. Everyone felt safe to discuss what their feelings were.

For Mom and Dad the meeting allowed them to take a step back and see what they were doing that contributed to Tommy's self-destructive behaviors. It also empowered them to see the changes in their son and the family due to some very simple adjustments to their parenting style.

Note

As parents we all have the best intentions for our children, but at times we may allow our personal expectations to interfere with the natural development of our children. It is important not to lose sight of the fact that they have their own unique journey. This journey allows for them to explore who they are, but not what we desire them to be. In this case Tommy's parents had lost sight of what they were doing. They really did not understand how their aggressive style of parenting was actually moving their son further away from the desired result as well as from the family as a whole.

CHAPTER 4

Understanding the Exceptional Child

The information here will provide a general understanding of the ADHD, (Attention Deficit Hyperactive Disorder), LD (Learning Disabled), and Learning Challenged child. Basically, all of these children have fallen into the same category and as you may or may not know, the symptoms and educational and social challenges all overlap.

Imagine living in a fast-moving merry-go-round where sounds, images and thoughts are constantly shifting. Where you may see letters, words or even numbers backwards, where you are easily bored and distracted at the same time. You are almost helpless to keep your mind on tasks you need to complete. You have difficulty remembering things that may have happened five seconds ago, let alone yesterday. You have difficulty organizing your thoughts and activities. Unimportant sights and sounds distract you; your mind drives you from one thought activity to the next. Sometimes you are so wrapped up in all of this turmoil that you do not notice when someone is speaking to you. It may be your teacher, parent or a friend. What you do feel is frustration, anger, confusion and fear that you do not learn or act as most of the others around you do. Your self-esteem is not good, you don't have self-confidence and your world does not feel safe to you at any time. A person with a learning disability lives with some, or all, of these symptoms on a daily basis.

Over the years ADHD has been given many names. ADHD is one of the most common learning and social disorders among children. Statistically, two to three times more boys than girls are affected. True attention deficit disorder is extremely rare, occurring in only 3 to 6 percent of the population. Unbelievably, it is now being estimated that the condition will be diagnosed in 20 percent of the population.

What now follows are some stories from children describing what it is like to have ADHD. You'll see and feel their frustrations as well as what their world is like moment to moment.

Biographies Written by the Exceptional Child

A note to the reader:
I have changed the names of the individuals depicted in these stories, but the stories themselves are representative of the children who I've worked with who exhibited symptoms of ADHD.

LEON - at 14 years of age

I have more energy than most boys my age. But then, I have always been overly active. Starting at age 3, I was a human tornado, dashing around and disrupting everything in my path. At home, I darted from one activity to the next, leaving a trail of toys behind me. At meals, I upset dishes and talked non-stop. I was reckless and people called me impulsive. Which I guess meant that I did not think before I acted. I ran into streets with oncoming cars and did many things to get me into trouble no matter how many times my mother explained the danger or punished me. On the playground, I desperately wanted to play with my friends. I couldn't understand why they stayed away from me. I felt "different" and got very angry many times and ended up getting into fights. My parents didn't know what to do. They tried to help, but I felt like I was all-alone on an island. It was scary. I wish things could have been different. I wish that I could have been normal. I wish..., I wish!

JESSICA - at age 17

I still struggle to pay attention and act appropriately. This has always been hard for me. I still get embarrassed thinking about the night that my parents took me out for my 10th birthday. I had gotten so distracted by the waitress' blonde hair that I didn't hear my father call out my name 3 times for me to order. Then, before I could stop myself I yelled out, "Your hair dye looks awful!"

I remember that in elementary and junior high school I was quiet and cooperative, but I daydreamed all of the time. Even though I was smart, I could never improve my grades no matter how hard I tried. I couldn't keep my mind on tests, failed quite often even though I knew most of the answers. My parents, not understanding what was happening to me, responded to my low grades by taking away privileges, calling me lazy and making me work harder. One day after failing yet another exam, my teacher found me sobbing. I told her that I was feeling worthless, dumb, depressed and all alone from my family and friends. "What's wrong with me?"... I cried!

LARRY - at age 8

I have trouble sitting in my seat. When a teacher asks a question, I get so excited that I jump out of my seat and yell out the answer. Even though she tells me to calm down, I can't control myself. I am always getting into trouble for talking and since I can never finish my class-work, I have to take it home and finish it as homework. My teacher makes me stay in at recess because I misbehave. I cannot read very well. I always mix up my letters so I work in a special group for reading. The teacher gives me headphones and I listen to tapes she says this helps me to pay attention.

I really don't understand all of this, although I know that I am different then my classmates. It makes me feel funny inside, not very smart and I get angry that my head does not seem to work properly. My parents tell me that I need to take medicine to help me learn better, so I do, but it actually makes me feel that there is something very wrong with me.

Identifying the Main Problems

The three people you have just met all have a form of Attention Deficit Hyperactive Disorder or Learning Disability. Unlike a cold or strep throat, these disorders do not have clear physical signs that can be diagnosed by a lab test. Looking for certain characteristic behaviors may only identify them and as you can see these behaviors vary from person to person.

The most common behaviors fall into 3 categories: inattention, hyperactivity and impulsiveness.

- **Inattention** – These children have a hard time keeping their mind on any one thing and may get bored with a task after only a few minutes. In contrast, they usually can spend huge amounts of time on activities that they enjoy, but focusing deliberate conscious attention to organize and complete a job or learning something new is difficult for them. For example, Jessica found it agonizing to do homework, often forgetting to write it down and bring home the necessary information. Also, every few minutes she found her mind drifting to something else. As a result she never finished her homework, which was always full of mistakes and there was constant warring with her parents.

- **Hyperactivity** – These children always seem to be in motion. Even when they seem to be still, their bodies, minds and mouths are always moving. They can't sit still. Like Leon, they dash around and are constantly jabbering away. Sitting still for longer than a few moments or even sometimes for a few seconds, can be an impossibility. Hyperactive children squirm in their seat, roam around the room, call out, need to have something in their hands, tap the desk, etc. You will notice that they will try to do several things at once, bouncing around from one activity to the next, while not completing anything.

- **Impulsiveness** – These children have difficulty controlling their immediate reactions. They have difficulty thinking before acting. As a result, like Jessica, they may blurt out inappropriate comments. You know the adage, "What we think, we usually say or do." In most of us we have the ability to control this impulse, but these children do not. Their impulsiveness may make it hard for them to wait for things they want or to take their turn in games. They may grab a toy from another child or hit someone when they are upset.

One may say that at times we all have some of these characteristics, so how do we assess whether our child has this disorder. Doctors, psychologists and educational specialists consider the following questions in making an assessment:

- Are these behaviors excessive or long term? Do they occur more often than in other people the same age?

- Are they a continuous problem, not just a response to a temporary situation?

- Do the behaviors occur in several different settings or only in one specific place?

These behaviors are compared with a set of criteria and characteristics, which appear in the reference book called *Diagnostic and Statistical Manual of Mental Disorders*.

What makes it so complex to diagnose is that many things can produce the above behaviors. For example, a formerly cooperative child who becomes overactive and easily distracted after a parent's death is dealing with an emotional problem. A child with chronic middle ear infections may also appear distracted and uncooperative, as can living with family members who are physically abusive or addicted to drugs or families that are going through separations and divorces. The divorce rate now is over 50%, do you wonder if there is any correlation between this and the behavioral characteristics that accompany ADHD? Can you imagine a child trying to focus on a reading or math lesson when they may be expending all of this energy in attempting to balance their emotions each day?

Suppose even, that the child has a learning disability and is not developmentally ready to learn how to read and write or work with numbers. Maybe the work is too hard, or maybe the materials have to be taught using different strategies or modalities.

We have seen that there are several different temperaments that a child may have and each one produces a different set of behaviors and in turn require handling in different ways. If situations are mishandled or not understood, there is a very good possibility that these children are showing the effects of other problems, and not ADHD.

Classroom Stories

Jerome shouted answers out in class, and then became disruptive when the teacher ignored him. He showed all of the symptoms of being hyperactive and impulsive. After observing Jerome in other situations, his teacher realized that he was just looking for some approval for knowing the right answer. Once the teacher shifted her behavior and gave Jerome more opportunities to answer with positive recognition, Jerome became an exemplary student.

Molly, a fourth grader made loud noises during reading group that disrupted the class. One day after spending some individual time with Molly, the teacher realized that the material was too hard for her. Molly's disruptions ceased when she was placed in a reading group, which was geared to her level of reading. She then began to participate with more success in the activity.

Other Disorders Which May Accompany ADHD

Many children with ADHD also have a specific learning disability ("LD"), this could manifest as having trouble with reading, math, writing skills or mastering language.

A small percentage of children have Tourette syndrome. Tourette symptoms come in the form of tics and other movements like eye blinks or facial twitches that cannot be controlled. People having this disorder may make strange sounds or have no control over their use of curse words. These behaviors can usually be controlled with medication.

Anxiety due to the tremendous stress these children are under usually manifests as anger. Their feelings of inadequacy for not having the ability to perform the assigned tasks, both at home and at school, compounded by the way they are seen by their peers in a social setting presents an amazing struggle which definitely impacts on their behavior and coping ability. A cause for concern should be noted here, as some of these children experience depression and suicidal tendencies. They are unable to see beyond their feelings of hopelessness. The symptoms of depression will show as constant disruption of sleep, loss of appetite or a severe increase in food intake or lack of the ability to perform daily responsibilities.

Understanding the Purpose of Your Child's Behavior

Try to discern the underlying reason for your child's behavior. Ask the who, what, when, where, how and why questions regarding whatever is going on at the time. Many times the responsibility for the behavior is incorrectly left with the child.

The undesirable behavior may be caused by some physical or chemical imbalance. It may be caused from some side effect of medication or from conflict between them and a teacher, friend or even an upset with you may be the cause of the problem.

It is important for all of us to know that behavior is a form of communication, even bad behavior. It becomes our responsibility to try to comprehend what it is our child is really trying to communicate to us, and then make any necessary changes to affect the appropriate solution.

Asking yourself some of the following questions will help you with this task.

Is your child asking for:

- A different type of structure. It may be more or less than is currently being applied. Sometimes your child needs more freedom than what is being given to them, and the opposite is true as well.

- More emotional support and reassurance.

- More movement and exercise.

- More (or less) stimulation, challenging work and experiences.

Could the behavior be in response to:

- Undue expectations, which cannot be met.

- Our style of dealing with the child. Maybe we are being too authoritative; maybe we are not listening carefully enough. Maybe we are not paying enough attention.

- A change within the family. Has there been a newborn? Are there marital problems going on. Has there been a move from one location to another.

Could the behavior be in reaction to:

- Criticizing the child in front of their friends.

- Insisting on a response before your child has the time to access the information or perform the activity.

- Teasing by friends or siblings.

- Being reprimanded for poor organization.

- Assigning a task, which is too difficult.

- Assigning a task, which is too repetitive and boring.

- Being given unclear directions.

As a parent, it is paramount that we become good listeners and observers and that we are cautious not to react too quickly, or before we know all of the underlying factors of a certain situation. We must practice first being introspective and then reacting on what it is our children are showing us that they really need.

Understanding Our Child

First and foremost we must remember that each child comes into this world as a unique individual. They are born as pure, unconditional loving, honest, trusting and open to the world and what it has to offer. Their uniqueness is further established through their interactions within the family and outside social issues.

There are however, some common elements in his or her humanness, which they share with others. Among the most important of these is the characteristic of being a social animal with a strong desire to have acceptance, to find their place in life, and to have a relationship with others that gives them a sense of identity and security.

Children's needs are very basic. They need to:

- Have a sense of physical and economic security.

- Love others and to be loved.

- Have a sense of personal worth.

- Experience life through their own mind, body and spirit.

We sometimes ask ourselves why our child does a certain thing. It is important to recognize that children do most of what they do to achieve social acceptance. Their desire is to be respected by, and to respect others. Accomplishing this creates a strong sense of self. Their behaviors are experiments in trying to discover what will bring recognition, acceptance and success. These are basic human needs and if we keep in mind, that what they are trying to do is fulfill these needs, we will realize the "why" of most of the behaviors our children display. They do what they do for the same reasons that we do. They want, need and indeed must have recognition, love and feelings of self-worth.

We can see in ourselves some of the ways in which we seek to satisfy these basic needs. We may recall, for example, a time when we have gone out of our way to make sure someone knew of an accomplishment, actually seeking to be complemented. Or, we may remember a time when we felt alone or depressed and we sought reassurance from a friend or family member. Children, also have a need to engage in behaviors that assure them they have a place or identity in their world. Children need this reassurance much more often than we think. Without us knowing it, much of a child's actions during the course of a day are aimed at satisfying these basic needs.

These feelings of love and worthiness give a child his/her sense of self and well being that we all aspire to attain in life. This basic identity is either positive, that is feeling a sense of success within oneself or negative, which is, feeling a sense of failure. Whether a child is gifted, ADHD or anywhere in between, to overcome a negative self-image or enhance a positive one, you must radiate unconditional love by showing acceptance, interest, being nonjudgmental and constantly encouraging them.

Differences in communication levels of children

Children love to play. This is how they interact with their world. Play is an excellent means of facilitating child expression. We see Therapists use play all the time to get children to communicate emotions, which they may be feeling.

Young children are straightforward and honest. They are extremely perceptive and pick up many nuances that are going on in the family that we don't realize. They are generally willing to discuss these perceptions openly. Our position is to respect their sophistication, be aware of their world and meet them on their level.

Children are typically more concrete in their communication. It is necessary to gear your vocabulary to your child's level of understanding. The use of concrete examples will be helpful for your child to grasp the meaning.

Early school years are challenging for them, as they are required for the first time to conform to group rules. This conforming often requires postponing immediate gratification. Sometimes pressure to conform also leads to conflict with authority figures.

Early school years also represent their first social experiences within a larger peer group. We know that while the peer group influence factor is an important one, and in most cases a positive influence, it can also create some negative behaviors. It will be helpful for you to know how your child reacts within his/her peer groups.

How We Can Communicate More Effectively With Our Child

This may sound harsh, but if we were to look at it, we would see that children seldom get the undivided positive attention of a concerned and compassionate adult. However, they do get our undivided attention when they have broken some rule. Consistent positive attention places us in a position of teaching the child more acceptable behaviors.

As a parent, we can enhance our effectiveness by being "Active Listeners". How frequently do we respond to our child's remarks before we truly understand what it is that they are saying to us? Our quick responses often reflect our own judgments more than they do the views our child is attempting to express.

What happens when the child perceives that they are not being understood are two-fold. First, they may try to express their point again or if it happens often enough, they will become discouraged and angry and stop attempting to communicate in an open way. They will try to find other ways to express these now frustrating and angry emotions. When this happens, a door between you and your child has closed. All in all, what these hasty responses create for your child is a feeling of non-acceptance and lack of respect.

An Active Listener:

- Is a person who listens and attends to the child with all of their senses tuned in to the moment.

- Hears what their child is saying and tries to determine what is going on in the moment.

- Will focus on the child and only interrupts for clarity when it is appropriate.

- Will focus primarily on the feelings of the child.

- Reflects to the child what they have heard in your own words. Then the child can verify your understanding of what they have said and the way in which you interpreted it.

Examples of Active Listening at Work

Alice: "All the kids tease me. Some of them even pull my hair".

Mom: "You feel like the other kids are giving you a pretty hard time"?

Carl: "I don't like my teacher, she is after me all of the time. "

Dad: "Wow, it sure looks like she is not one of your favorite people".

Janet: "I don't want to do that today".

Dad: "Ahhh, I see you're not very excited about doing your homework today, right?"

In each of these cases, the parent is validating their child's feelings and has left the door open for the child to continue the discussion. These open statements place the burden of responding on the child. Have you heard any of these door openers:

- "Tell me about it"

- "I see"

- "No fooling"

- "MMMMMMM tell me more"

- "Oh, this seems like something important to you"

Very often we get caught up in the 'I' and 'YOU' messages e.g.,

I-message - "I feel really upset now."

You-message - "You've really messed up. "

It is through honest 'I' messages that we can share feelings with our child. We may have to be patient with our child at the beginning (i.e., listening to our "I" messages) because a child's major concern is himself. The child's world is one of necessity and discovery, gradually, with maturation and patience a child begins to realize that others have feelings too. As a parent you are showing them how to care and understand who they are. They will then be able to give it back to you. Gradually, a child learns that when you share with them, it means that he/she is important and worthy of your confidence and respect. Sharing with your child can be seen as one of the highest forms of acceptance.

A wise person once told me that with children we share our feelings, not our burdens. Not to unburden ourselves, but to give of ourselves. Honesty, simplicity and brevity and a lot of discernment will make your 'I' messages very effective.

Ways to Facilitate Communication

These can be called attending behaviors and can prove effective with all of our social contacts:

- Have eye contact. Be in a position to make eye contact. If it is not happening, gently bring their chin up to your face and teach them how to do it back to you when they feel you are slipping. Praise them when your eyes meet each other. There is a tremendous and very powerful exchange that takes place when you look at each other. You can tell a lot about a person through their eyes.

- Physical posture. Place yourself on the same level as your child. This may mean sitting in a small chair, perhaps on the floor or any way that puts you on equal levels. This indicates respect and a desire to communicate.

- It is important to express your desires and feelings through your tone of voice. A lot can be discerned through how you say things. Through this your child learns and feels compassion, love, limits, anger, frustration, judgments etc. It is up to us to decide how we wish to express ourselves and what we want to teach to our child.

Probably the most important thing of all is to remember that our children are our teachers. They will teach us what their needs are through their interactions with us. Follow their lead, allow for them to teach us about who they are and what their needs might be. Let them teach us about who we are by how they see us interacting with them. It is our responsibility to create a more communicative atmosphere between our child and ourselves.

Just by being good observers and listeners our job becomes an easier one.

Facilitating Better Interaction With Our Child

Qualities of love, communication, emotions and the desire for knowledge in our little ones, can be nurtured by:

- Teaching them self-acceptance through acknowledgment for the things that they do well. Always accentuate the positive aspects of their behavior. This allows for your child to identify with positive traits and characteristics about themselves.

- Being a mirror to your child's feelings, (e.g., "You seem especially happy today, Lisa). This helps them identify and discuss what is going on in their life.

- Teaching independence and self-control by allowing

your child to experiment and take risks in situations where you know that no harm will come to them. This reinforces new discoveries within their world.

- Allowing them to set their own goals and once they have achieved them, let them know that you know they did a good job.

- Allowing them to make decisions for themselves and take responsibility for those decisions. This enables them to see consequences, both good and bad, which allows for them to make decisions to change the direction they are going in. Through your guidance, rather than control, you allow for them to develop their own paths.

- Learning to respond effectively. For example you may say, "Sometimes I feel good just thinking about my friend". The expectation is that as your relationship strengthens, the child will behave more as you behave.

As a parent it is important to have patience and understanding during the process. Remember development happens in stages. Sometimes moving slowly, sometimes more rapidly. Each child is unique and travels their journey at their own pace. We must be careful of high expectations and allow for them to come to their own realizations.

Characteristics that Grow Relationships
Genuineness

The ability to be open and honest is essential in

the development of any relationship. It nurtures trust and a general feeling of well being within us. Try to recognize those times that you are being honest with yourselves. You should also recognize a feeling of satisfaction. This is very healing both for yourself and your child. Make this the only acceptable way in which you and your child communicate with each other.

Understanding

How much you are aware of, and understand your own feelings can be determinative of your capacity for understanding what another person is going through and how you chose to respond to them under that particular circumstance. Compassion and empathy are learned behaviors, usually resulting from how we were treated, or wished to be treated under tumultuous circumstances.

Valuing

To what extent do we see others and ourselves as being worthy of respect as human beings? How much do we value who we really are? Very often we will allow for our expectations to interfere with this, resulting in our being disappointed and angry.

Observe how you interact with pets. With them we are open, accepting and have very few expectations of them. You respect them for who they are. What you give them, you get back. The same can be said for the way we treat our children, our neighbors and ourselves.

Acceptance

This is the degree to which you allow yourself, or other people to be themselves, to have their own opinions, ideas and feelings and the extent to which you allow them to express their own individuality. This has to be done unconditionally and without any expectations. This is where we explore the degree of freedom we give to ourselves as well. Make a list of all of the guidelines and limits that you place on yourself, on your emotions, on your ability to express your own creativity. Each new rule creates another layer or wall that we choose to hide behind rather than allowing it to come out in our character. Each layer removes a tiny bit of the TRUE freedom we have. The TRUE freedom that we have taken away from ourselves and then cannot pass on to others.

The communication of love, genuineness, understanding, and acceptance can be done in many ways. We do it with words, tone of voice, body language, but mostly thorough our attitude. More important than anything else is the basic attitude that you bring to the interaction that you have with your child. If you recognize that children need only the proper guidance to develop into successful adults, then this is what will be communicated to the child. Your positive attitude will enable you to have a strong and positive relationship with your child.

Emergence

This next passage is about emergence. No matter who we are, where we are in our life, or what our family life might be like, we all have the ability to transform. To see, feel, and be part of the beauty no matter what our journey might be.

Caterpillar/Butterfly

By Alice Brownlee & Howard Jerome

I creep I crawl. I never think of the sky at all.
I inch around eating the food that I find on the ground.
I'm not what you'd call a thriller.
I'm a **fuzzy** Caterpillar.

Suddenly something strange occurs to me.
And pretty soon, I crawl on a leaf and I spin a cocoon.
I feel like I am transforming, A brand new me is a borning.

I'm still alive. I have the power to survive.
I know it's true, you have this power inside you.
I push, I kick; It's starting to tear; I've learned the trick.
Suddenly, one last push and I'm finally free.

I'm hanging here, I'm exhausted, but I'm free, it's worth what it costed.

My fuzz is gone. I've only six legs to carry me on.
And who am I? I've gone through a change and I'm wondering why.

Look, I'm pink and it's shocking, are these my knees that are knocking?

I breathe, I sigh, the sun is warm, I start to dry.
A bluebird sings and look at me I've grown new wings.
I flit, I fly, I land on a flower, then head for the sky.
I sail, I sip, I'm drinking nectar, sure is a trip.

This sure beats creeping and crawling, you too can fly, stop your stalling.
Come flap your wings and feel the joy that freedom can bring.
Come fly with me and pretty soon you too will agree,
It's such a marvelous feeling freedom is OH so appealing.

It's up to you to do the things you're born to do....
And pretty soon you too will break your own cocoon.
So farewell, adieux, I'm happy I met each one of you.
I hope some day, our paths will cross and we will fly and play.

Doo, doo, dee, dee, doo, doo, doo, doo, dee, dee, dee, dee doo!!

CHAPTER 5

Medications used in the Treatment of the Exceptional Child

"There is No Magic" is designed to offer you, as the parent or custodian, various alternatives which will maximize your special needs child's educational and social development. It is also about helping you make the best choices for both you and your family.

The issue of the use of medication presents a huge dilemma. On one hand, we know that medication is not the answer, yet on the other hand, in many cases our medical practitioners and school systems say there is no other alternative if your child is to be maintained in the classroom. This really becomes a crossroad of choices for you, your child and the entire family. It is probably one of the most important decisions that you will make in the life of your child.

Although the information here will present both sides, I believe that you will see that I do have a bias against the usage of medication. Even though there are definitely times and places for its use, my feeling is that the dispensing of medication to manage your child is being overused.

As you are reading this chapter keep in mind that the disability ADHD comes in different forms. The "H" in ADHD is for HYPERACTIVITY. The treatment for this neuro-biological disability is different than we may treat the traditional Attention Deficit Disorder Child. In this case we may be more apt to use medication (among other management tools) to help slow down the pace of the child, whereas the choices used for the treatment of the NON-HYPERACTIVE child may be entirely different and preclude the use of medication. I do believe that we are presently using medication as a quick fix, and have taken away very serious ethical and spiritual choices from you as the parent, but more importantly, from your special needs child.

Medication and ADHD

People with ADHD have problems with impulse control, initiative, motivation, and attention to routines and prioritization of tasks and organization. Medications used for treating ADHD elevate the levels of neurotransmitters in the parts of the brain that affect these activities. Neurotransmitters are chemicals the brain cells use to communicate with each other.

There are three types of medications that are helpful with the symptoms of ADHD. These include stimulants, anti-depressants and medicines used for treating high blood pressure.

1.   ***Stimulants***   These are the most commonly used medications. This group includes Ritalin, Adderall, Dexedrine and Cylert. Stimulants work very quickly. They are called stimulants because they give a person enough "mental energy" to focus on what they are doing. They often require multiple doses during the day. Cylert is the exception to this rule. It usually is only taken once per day.

Side Effects: The three most frequent side effects of stimulants are poor appetite, trouble getting to sleep and weight loss. This can usually be controlled by changes in the dosage of medication.

Some parents and teachers notice that children on stimulants lose their spontaneity. The child may even look depressed. Adjustments in the dosage usually show an improvement in these symptoms.

Headaches and stomachaches may occur. They often go away after the patient becomes accustomed to the dosage. Two rare side effects that may be seen are tics and growth delay. Tics usually come in the form of facial twitches. They may occur in about two to three percent of the cases and almost always disappear after the dosage is adjusted.

2. ***Antidepressants*** They tend to help decrease mood swings. They take longer to start working and have more risks associated with them. Wellbutrin is a common antidepressant used in the treatment of ADHD. Others are Effexor and Tofranil.

   Side Effects: Common symptoms are drowsiness, dry mouth irritability and sleep disturbance. These side effects are rare and usually temporary. Anti-depressants have the potential to cause seizures. Wellbutrin has a higher seizure rate than the others, but in its sustained release capsule form it has shown a significantly lower seizure rate.

3. ***Anti-hypertensives*** Two medications used for treating high blood pressure, Clonidine and Tenex are sometimes added to stimulants when they are not fully effective in reducing the hyperactivity, impulsiveness or aggression. They are rarely used alone to treat ADHD.

Side Effects: The most common side effects include tiredness and dizziness. Elevation of blood pressure, rapid heart beat and flu like symptoms (diarrhea, runny nose) has been observed.

Some Basic facts about ADHD Medications

For decades, stimulant medications have been used to treat the symptoms of ADHD. For many people, these medicines reduce their hyperactivity and improve their ability to focus, work and learn. The medications may also improve physical coordination, such as handwriting and the skills required in athletic activities.

- Stimulant drugs such, as Ritalin, Dexedrine and Aderall, when used under medical supervision are safe. They can be addictive to teenagers and adults if misused.

- Ritalin and Dexedrine come in short-term tablets that last about four hours, as well as longer time released capsules that will stay effective during the school day.

- Nine out of ten children improve on one of the stimulant drugs. So if one doesn't help, or is showing signs of one of the side effects, other ones may be tried. Usually, a medication should be tried over a period of time to see if there are any observable changes in the behavior of the child. When necessary, the doctor may try adjusting the dosage of a drug prior to switching to a different drug altogether.

- Other types of medication may be used if stimulants are not effective. Antidepressants and other medications may be used to help control accompanying anxiety or depression. Clonidine, a drug normally used to treat hypertension has been found helpful with people who have ADHD or Tourette syndrome. Although stimulants tend to be more effective, Clonidine may be used in conjunction with the stimulant when additional symptoms such as a tic disorder is present.

- The doctor should work closely with each patient to find the most appropriate medication and dosage. As a parent, when you decide to use a form of drug therapy with your child, you should make sure that the child is getting the prescribed daily dosage both at home and in the school to ensure positive and accurate results.

- Typical challenges that children face, such as changes in their routine; dramatic changes within the family or home structure; or entering puberty, are exaggerated for the ADHD child.

- During times when the child is not required to be in complete control of his/her behavior (vacations), you may wish to discontinue the use of medication to allow the body a break from the effects of the drug. Also, your Doctor may recommend that the child be taken off of the medication at different stages of your child's development to see if they are still in need of it.

- Children who are on medications should have regular checkups. You should also talk regularly with the child's teacher and your doctor about any positive/negative changes in the behavior or physical condition of the child.

The Medication Debate

As useful as these drugs are, Ritalin and the other stimulants have sparked a great deal of controversy. Most doctors feel that the potential side effects from the drugs should be carefully weighed against the benefits before prescribing this form of treatment. As previously mentioned, while on these medications, some children may lose weight, have less appetite and temporarily grow at a slower rate. Others may have problems with their sleep patterns. Early Studies revealed that stimulants may make the symptoms of Tourette syndrome worse, although more recent research rebuts this theory altogether. As a parent, it is natural to be concerned about whether taking medicine is in your child's best interest. One needs to be clear about the benefits and potential risks of using these drugs.

Another debate is whether Ritalin and other stimulant drugs are prescribed unnecessarily for too many children. It is important to remember that many things, including anxiety, depression, allergies, or problems within the home or school environment can make children seem overactive, impulsive and inattentive. Critics argue that many children who do not have true Attention Deficit Disorder are medicated as a way to control their disruptive behavior.

Also to be noted, when a child's schoolwork and behavior improve soon after starting medication, parents and teachers tend to applaud the drug for causing the sudden change. We may be forgetting that these changes are actually the child's own strengths and natural abilities coming out. Giving credit to the medication can disempower the child and actually add to their feeling of insecurity and self-consciousness. The medication only facilitates the possibility of these changes. It is the child who is supplying the effort and ability, and needs to be recognized for this by parents and teachers alike.

A Case Study

Each case study depicted throughout these chapters are actual experiences that parents and their children have gone through. Please take note that as individuals and families we are a work in progress. As individuals we are able to deal with our issues at whatever level we are on in our developmental growth and the same holds true for our children. Remember, that there is no absolute right or wrong way of handling problems or situations. If you truly can believe this then there is no shame or guilt that accompanies any behavior which results from decisions that are made. There is also no need for judgments whether they are our own or those that we feel others are making of us. What is significant are our observations and decisions that we make in the moment. That we empower our children and ourselves by being able to create our own map of our own unique journey.

All the names that appear within the pages of this book are fictitious

Les - The Misdiagnosed Child
History

I first met Les when he was 7 1/2, when I was asked to get involved with his diagnosis of Attention Deficit and Hyperactive Disorder.

He had been seen by his family doctor and described as ADHD with anxiety. It was indicated that he showed characteristics of avoidance when faced with challenges or tedious tasks. His low frustration tolerance triggered a rapid escalation of anxiety which manifested in verbal explosiveness with threats and a potential to be violent. He was noted to flee, hide and sometimes show physical aggression.

Les had already been removed from two schools, one being his Pre-Kindergarten within a Public School and again in his Kindergarten class in a private Montessori school. Both were for the same reason, that due to his impulsivity and potential explosiveness, which had led to physical encounters with his teachers and classmates, he could not be contained in an open classroom structure.

Desired outcomes:

The recommendations coming from the school were:

1. Confirmation of Diagnosis for "Exceptional" behavior.

2. Application for a Self-Contained class structure.

3. One to one support.

4. Possible placement in a Day Treatment Program designed for children with severe emotional and social dysfunctions.

5. Administration of Ritalin to control Les' impulsive and aggressive behaviors.

His parents were understandably quite upset and frustrated, as they no longer felt like they had a handle on the situation. At home Les did not exhibit these behaviors to the same degree. My personal observation was that he was a very intelligent, sensitive and personable boy. His mother indicated that although he did have episodes where he had tantrums, these had diminished significantly over recent months and that presently there existed few problems at home.

Mom had indicated that about 12 months previous she had become quite ill with her pregnancy of her second child. It was during this time that Les started to exhibit some aggressive behavior both at home and at school.

My observations

It was my opinion that Les became very afraid that his mother was not going to recover and due to his extreme sensitivity carried this concern with him. It was at school though, where his anxieties heightened because in his mind she was still sick. Consequently Les appeared to be on the edge. At times when he was under stress, he was not able to contain himself very well.

It should be noted that mom had regained her health after the birth and although she tried to convey this to Les, he was not able to believe it.

I spent several sessions with the family as a whole and found them to be a loving and caring family and that Les did not portray a picture of a child with Attention Deficit Disorder during any of my visits. He and I had many play sessions together and he exhibited all of the personality traits of a normal, healthy, responsible and highly intelligent child.

I observed that Les was a child that was operating on two very different levels of personality. One at home and the other at school. We were faced with having both the medical and the school institutions lobbying to label this child as having social and academic dysfunctions based upon his behavior with them.

I also observed that this was an extremely sensitive child who had a legitimate fear that the school environment could not provide him with a safe and secure place to be, learn and grow in.

Results

There was 3 months left in the school year when Les was asked to leave. His parents decided to keep him at home where he received home instruction. During that time he was enrolled in a new school that was just being built within his neighborhood.

The following plan was implemented during this time:

- We met with the new principal on several occasions so that an appropriate teacher and classroom could be chosen.

- Plans were laid to have a special full time aid trained to implement a social and academic plan for Les.

- We worked with the school support team to develop a behavioral plan designed to reinforce his emotional needs and redevelop his trust for the school and his teachers, whom he had felt abandoned by on other occasions.

Once school started, we began to see immediate progress as Les responded to the warm, sensitive and caring approach from his new teachers.

Note

It was obvious from the start that another look had to be taken at the diagnosis of ADHD. There were too many other possible contributing factors for Les' behavior. We decided to do a test run of no medication to see if there were any significant changes to his behavior. He displayed no signs of returning to his previous behavior when taken off the medication.

Although Les originally had not responded within the same limits and rules as most other children, the combination of trained personnel and their patience created a new experience for Les to operate in. Each time he tested their authority it was met with firmness, consistency and love, a much different experience then the anger and impatience his previous experiences offered to him.

Les developed a new sense of confidence and trust.

Within 3 months his aid was cut back to half the time and by the end of the school year was just there for him to talk to when he needed to.

The next school year his self-esteem and confidence were strong enough so that he did not require any special support. Needless to say he was in a much better position to perform at or above his social and academic levels.

"Ritalin"
A Wonder Drug, or a Crutch

Did you Know?

This drug is a class 2 narcotic. In the prescribing information for Ritalin shown in the Physician's Desk Reference, the manufacturer, Ciba-Geigy, acknowledges that it does not know how Ritalin works, nor does it know how its effects relate to the condition of the central nervous system.

> *"There is neither specific evidence which clearly establishes the mechanism whereby Ritalin produces its' mental and behavioral effects in children, nor conclusive evidence regarding how these effects relate to the condition of the central nervous system."*

Under the heading of WARNINGS it states,

"Ritalin should not be used in children under six years, since safety and efficacy in this age group has not been established".

Parents and educators are often told that the standard drug therapy for ADHD revolves around four major stimulants: Ritalin, Dexedrine, Desoxyn and Cylert. According to research these stimulant medications are shown to have a 60-80 percent short-term effectiveness in controlling symptoms such as hyperactivity, distractibility and impulsivity in school-age children. It is said that the drug improves academic achievement in children by helping them to increase their attention spans and to decrease their disruptive and acting out behaviors. These stimulant medications are known to have a calming effect, which usually lasts for approximately four hours per dosage.

When these stimulants fail to control behavior, antidepressants such as Prozac or Anafranil are used to reduce anxiety levels and socially unacceptable behaviors.

At times drugs such as Clonidine are also used for their calming effects and to improve the sleep cycle.

Researchers are now talking about the extremely dangerous effect drug therapy can have both physically and psychologically on our children, and of course psychologically on parents. With emotional disorders striking an estimated 13% of children, and the increase of the amount of drugs available to treat depression, pharmacological researchers say prescriptions such as Prozac and Zoloft are increasing at an alarming rate. A national study found that doctors prescribed, recommended or administered antidepressants to children (birth to age 18) 4. 6 million times in 1992.

Does this sound like something that is beneficial to both you and your child? Can this prescription become addictive to both you and your child? Do we need to be drugging our children, or can we deal with certain learning, social and behavioral issues through alternative means? These are some impactful questions, which we should be asking of ourselves.

Studies done in the 1996, Journal of American Medical Association, reveal that in the past decade, there is more than a 300 percent increase in the number of school age children receiving stimulant medication.

Though well-meaning medical experts are under an enormous amount of pressure from teachers, parents and schools to make a diagnosis for children with these ADHD symptoms and then to treat them with prescription drugs as the preferred mode of treatment.

Dr. Peter Breggin, a psychiatrist and the author of "The War Against Children", says that Ritalin is dangerously over-prescribed, and without a doubt I would concur with this assessment. These drugs most definitely have side effects. Among these common side effects are anxiety, nausea, headaches and weight loss. Other side effects noted were high blood pressure, increased heart rate and Tourette syndrome.

Peter S. Jensen, head of the children's disorders research branch of the National Institute of Mental Health, called misdiagnosis and inappropriate drug treatment of children *"a critical public health concern"*. *"Many of the problems being addressed by medication are conditions of life*", adds Cheston Berlin, head of the American Academy of Pediatrics committee on drugs.

I believe that there is a correlation between the decrease in special education funding and the increase in the use of Ritalin. With the tremendous decline in programming and support for children with learning problems, there are fewer special educational teachers available to the school systems. Resources and designated classrooms, which were supporting children with special needs, have become few and far between. Children with learning deficits are now usually placed into large classrooms, without adequate educational or emotional support, and are left there to find their own way through their educational experience.

When considering treatment and interventions for ADHD, many teachers and parents are abdicating their professional judgment in favor of a medical model. They may go along with a pharmacological solution just because of the lack of support that exists within the public school system to institute alternative solutions to help maintain the condition.

There are no sure-fire methods for diagnosing ADHD. General practitioners and pediatricians use a one to two page questionnaire to determine a diagnosis prior to prescribing psycho-pharmacological drugs for the maintenance of the said condition. I remember, not to long ago, when every child would have had to undergo extensive testing and psychological evaluation before any medication would ever be considered, let alone prescribed, and then it was only used as a last resort form of treatment.

Is this what we as parents and educators are choosing as a viable means of keeping our children "under control"? Is this what we want to teach our children, that a pill is the answer to achieving normalcy and greater success in school and in life? Is this the way to develop their inner confidence and self-esteem? Or, are we as parents and educators, trying to find the easy, most convenient way out?

Researchers concur that medication alone is not enough. They say that treatment with stimulant medication does not increase academic achievement over the long term. At the very least, children with academic and social difficulties need individualized and well-planned educational programs that address the specific educational, behavioral, psychological, and pharmacological needs of the individual child.

Many of the ADHD children in the mainstream educational system, are taking medication without having any access to supplemental or supportive interventions. Exercise and nutritional programs, would at least assist them with their condition, if not alleviate the need for taking a mood-altering drug, altogether.

The question then arises, "are these drugs being used as a tool to control and manage behavior in the classroom and at home"?

Parents are often told that by placing their children on stimulant medication, they will be helping them academically and socially. However, is there confirming data available to support this claim? On the contrary. As a matter of fact, there is growing data and information to support the need for holistic alternatives to treat these conditions. Many of which will be discussed in future chapters, right here, so stay tuned!!

What can you as parents do to help your children cope in today's environment?

Here are a few recommendations:

You need to be patient and only consent to the use of stimulant medication as a last resort. You can do this by:

- Making sure that a comprehensive academic and management program that meets the individual needs of your child are in place at your school.

- That the goals of your child's Individualized Educational Plan (IEP) are looked at regularly by yourself and school staff, and are adjusted whenever necessary.

- That an educational and behavioral management program plan is in place at home, designed to parallel and support the program within the school.

You can consult with an educational specialist who can work with you and the school (if necessary) in designing a program that takes into account the existing academic, social and psychological needs of your child.

You can opt to place your child in an independent school where there is usually a lower student to teacher ratio, and where there may be a program geared to the individual needs of your child.

As we move along here and you see the various alternatives that you as a parent have, you will also see the need to be proactive participants in every aspect of your child's education. Such partnering used to be standard procedure. Why would we accept less from our school system at this critical juncture? It may be time to insist that they administer this standard once again.

CHAPTER 6

How We Learn

In The Beginning

Our time of learning begins at a point just after conception. As our heart begins beating and our brain starts developing we become aware of our first living environment. Our sense of hearing, sight and touch are beginning to operate as well. We begin sensing emotions and hearing sounds, all of which are beginning to make impressions on us. Our environment is warm, safe and we begin to feel our first sensations of security. We grow accustomed to this, and become familiar with every nook and cranny of our gestational home. We feel love and nurturing from Mom as she massages the womb area and coos to us at every opportunity. Everything that flows through the veins and arteries of mom flows through ours. If she keeps herself physically healthy, we are healthy. If she takes drugs, we take drugs. If she listens to Mozart, we sense it. If she listens to Rock and Roll we sense that as well. If she is a happy and emotionally well-balanced person we learn from this attitude she has of herself and are likely to incorporate the same, or similar aspects into our own personality with ours. If she is living with stress, anger, or frustration we can sense this instability and this as well can leave its' impression on us.

In a sense, at the time of conception we have already come to life.

Every single moment that we are alive we are in a constant state of learning. We learn through our mind and body connection. Each of us has a spirit unique to us. This spirit, as gentle as it may seem, is an entity unto itself, experimenting, asking questions, watching, listening and expanding. It is always striving for the ultimate feeling of knowing itself completely, being happy and content with itself, loving and nurturing itself, of being one with itself.

We are born into the physical world as pure, open, innocent and loving beings. Our love is unconditional. We are ready to begin our journey in this lifetime. The journey of becoming "who we were meant to be". We want to give, we want to receive, we want to experience, and we want to make our own decisions. This constant transitioning is what helps to create a responsible, loving, respectful and understanding individual. This individuality we create for ourselves is represented in our self-esteem, our uniqueness, our freedom, ... in who we really are.

Ways in Which We Learn

One of the miracles of being human is our ability to learn. As we look at each and every living thing on this earth we can see that it learns to survive on this planet by using all the means that it has been provided in order for it to flourish.

We have identified three basic sensory modalities that we use to process information to memory. These are Visual, Auditory, and Kinesthetic (learning by doing). There is also a fourth, Tactile (hands on experience).

We generally rely on one predominant modality, but some of us have a balance between two, or even three of these traits.

Although all of us share these same senses, the way in which we apply them in order to perceive, understand, or retain and recall information, is unique to us. This recognition emphasizes the need to find out what your child's learning strengths are. Once we have ascertained this information, we are better prepared to individualize our child's educational program, both at home and in the school.

The Visual Learner

The most common form of learning is visual. A visual learner is someone who learns best by using their ability to visualize when processing information. This can be done through pictures, charts, diagrams, and videos or by watching a demonstration. If you are a visual learner, you will like to picture things in your mind, you remember faces even though you forget the names that goes with them. It's likely that you prefer to watch an activity before doing it yourself.

How to spot a Visual Learner

- This child likes to look at the pictures and drawing within a book.

- They need to see it to know it.

- They like to keep things in an orderly manner. Their surroundings are usually very neat and organized.

- They remember where they have seen things and are good at finding things that have been misplaced.

- They have an acute ability to focus on details, e.g., how you dress, what color your eyes are, misspellings.

- They do not follow directions well when given orally.

- They will enjoy playing with puzzles.

- They like to watch people's faces.

- They have a strong sense of color.

- They generally have artistic abilities.

- Excessive noise and sounds may bother them.

- They are better at math reasoning than computation.

- They read maps well.

- They learn sight words better than phonics.

- They must visualize words in order to spell them.

- They have excellent long-term memory.

- They prefer the computer to handwriting.

- They like to develop their own methods for problem solving.

- They arrive at correct solutions intuitively. They are good at seeing the "whole picture".

- Because they learn by seeing, they are sensitive to people's attitudes.

- They are likely mechanically, creatively or emotionally gifted.

Enhancing the performance of the visual learner

- Modify their environmental stimuli by having their areas as uncluttered as possible.

- Highlight areas on their worksheet, to help them see one item at a time.

- Give one step of an assignment at a time.

- They learn by experience. When giving them a project it is best to give them the entire picture and then break it down into smaller steps.

Tips for the Visual Learner

- Use of graphics to reinforce learning (pictures, slides, films and diagrams).

- Give demonstrations and allow them to practice for confirmation that they understood.

- Color-coding to organize information and their possessions.

- Teach using games, charts and graphs.

- Write down directions.

- Use dictionaries, and when teaching this child to read give visual symbols for sounds.

- Use flashcards.

- Filmstrips, movies and television are effective learning tools as well.

The Auditory Learner

Auditory learners learn most efficiently by hearing the material. They may be more talkative than the visual learner because they have a tendency to "think out loud".

They learn best by listening to audiotapes and participating within discussion groups.

How to spot an Auditory learner

- They love to talk, try to be funny by telling jokes.

- They are great storytellers and can become very creative when reciting their version of a story.

- They have poor handwriting with a history of reversing their "b's" and "d's"

- They remember what is said to them and can repeat it with amazing accuracy.

- They tend to have poor performances on group intelligence tests. They perform better when questions are read out loud.

- They learn by trial and error.

- They are analytical thinkers and they attend well to details.

- They are good at math.

- They have good short-term memory and are well organized.

What can be done to enhance the performance of the Auditory learner

- Take out as much noise from their workspace as possible.

- Use as few words as possible when giving directions.

- Speak directly to the child.

- Soft background music to drown out outside stimuli may help when doing homework.

- Earphones and tape recorders help cut out the distractions of other noises.

Tips for the Auditory Learner

- Teach them how to talk through a task. Repeat it to them for confirmation.

- Allow them to spell out loud.

- When learning how to read, allow for them to say their sounds and words out loud. They may have to read out loud to help them with their comprehension.

- Encourage oral responses and presentations.

- In school, pair them up with a visual learner so they can compensate for each other.

- They learn well through music and television.

- Auditory tapes are effective learning tools.

The Kinesthetic Learner

These children can be divided up into two categories, tactile for children who learn better through touching and kinesthetic for children who learn better by doing. Their performances are heightened through touch, movement and manipulation. The kinesthetic child needs to move, it is what they do best. They love to touch and socialize. They are adept at activities such as dance, arts and crafts and the use of the computer. He/she should be placed in a classroom with a teacher who uses hands–on teaching techniques. They love drama. Your child will be stifled and miserable with a teacher who emphasizes sitting quietly and learning specifically through the visual or auditory modalities.

How to spot a Kinesthetic Learner

- They are quite active and like to touch and feel everything.

- They are very good mechanically as they can take things apart and put them back together again.

- They are well coordinated and athletic.

- They are generally classified as underachievers.

- They enjoy doing experiments.

- They make physical contact with people when talking to them.

- They may seem to be very disorganized.

- They may have trouble memorizing lists and numbers.

What can be done to enhance the performance of the kinesthetic learner

- They enjoy role-playing and acting.

- They like the challenge of problem solving activities.

- Field trips are great for them.

- Make lists for them.

- Use props to explain concepts.

Tips for the Kinesthetic Child

- Athletic activities work well with the kinesthetic child. Group activities such as baseball, football, soccer, hockey or basketball. Individual sports such as swimming, gymnastics, skating, tennis, martial arts, yoga.

- Dance is especially great for the kinesthetic child. The combination of stretching, movement and music fine-tunes every aspect of the individual. Learning the routines balances the left and right hemispheres of the brain. It strengthens the mind/body connection as well as building well-coordinated bodies.

- Crafts of all forms appeal to the kinesthetic child. You will have hours of fun and quality time with your child.

- Cooking may fit in well with this child and may be one type of teaching practice used since it teaches things such as math, science, and reading and in a hands-on way, allows them to experience it in a fun way.

- Computers and video games are a favorite for the kinesthetic child. They use their well-tuned fine-motor coordination and good eye-hand coordination with these activities. Look for software that uses these skills while teaching educational concepts. Another favorite activity of kinesthetic children is chatting on-line as they get to talk with their hands.

- They love to build and fix things. The feeling of satisfaction and pride your child gains from this is priceless. They are very adept at it, so once they get started don't be surprised to see many mechanical appliances in various stages of repair.

- They have a wonderful imagination and love to participate in drama activities. Don't be surprised if they ask you if they can take acting lessons.

Setting the Stage for Learning

Children who have difficulties with learning can receive assistance in the regular classroom in numerous ways. Teacher's aids, peer tutoring, modified curriculums are available to supplement the basics of classroom teaching.

Statistics indicate that individuals experiencing difficulties within the school structure are more apt to fail. We know that if someone fails a task often enough, he or she will find the task adverse and avoid it altogether. Because so many of our kids find a large portion of schoolwork difficult and often experience the frustration of failure, they can be expected to engage in a good deal of escape behaviors such as simply avoiding the work and finding ways to attract negative attention to themselves.

Therefore, it becomes essential that both our home and school settings be designed to maximize their opportunities for success.

- Maintain a supportive and stress free environment so that the student is free to learn both socially and academically. As parents and teachers, it is our attitude and approach that creates the climate for our kids. If we are positive, the child will take a more constructive approach to his/her responsibilities. The opposite is true as well. A negative environment will affect the performance and behavior of the child. If the child does not feel emotionally safe, they will experience anxiety, frustration and anger. These feelings will decrease attention and concentration and inhibit the learning process.

- Individual modifications need to be accommodated into the plan. Nothing succeeds like success. The best way to motivate children is to design their programs to ensure their best efforts will result in success.

- Children need to tangibly see their successes. Graphs are good tools whereby the child sees exactly how they are doing on a specific task. Providing frequent praise increases the likelihood that the child will wish to behave in a positive manner.

- Allow for your child to see that you are a partner and have a vested interest in seeing them succeed. That you advocate for them at home and at school. Doing this will increase their feelings of security, which in turn increases their self-esteem and allows for them to continue moving forward.

- Be a good role model. Remember that even though they may have difficulty focusing at times, their eyes are always watching you.

Learning Within the Home Environment

As previously discussed, our educational system and the way that our special needs child is being taught has drastically changed during the past 10 years. It has left us confused as to exactly what is being done to ensure how these children are actually being taught. One thing we definitely need to do is take on an active role in the education of our child both within the school and at home.

To do this we must have a good understanding of:

- The strengths and weaknesses of our child;

- Which learning modalities our child learns best by; and

- The temperament of our child and how to best handle them in stressful situations.

We must be prepared to become qualified instructors to them in the home. Let's not fool ourselves though, this can, and will present its own challenges. Here are some of the issues that you are probably facing on a daily basis:

Distractibility – cannot keep on task when given an assignment.

Frustration – no tolerance when given a task that is confusing or repetitious.

Boredom – easily bored with repetitive tasks, like spelling, handwriting or math facts.

Clueless – You will experience times where the information just cannot sink in.

Noise – Outside stimuli of other siblings playing or chattering away, create an inability to concentrate and stay focused.

The key is to find out what educational and management strategies work best for you and your child. This takes some research and a lot of experimentation. As time goes by you will develop strategies of your own that will clearly make a difference.

Some of the following tactics have proven successful in helping a child to focus when they may be feeling antsy or are easily distracted:

- **Have them exercise first**

  You will be amazed at how, after a rigorous exercise program, your child will be much more focused and better prepared to do their work (refer to Chapter 7 on exercise).

- **Have them do two things at once**

  Sometimes we think that when our kids are off daydreaming or turned upside down in a chair or grabbing at flies from the air, then they must not be listening. In many cases, not only are they listening, but they are so under challenged by what is being taught that they decide to use their time wisely by taking on even more tasks in order to keep themselves busy and stimulated.

Many do much better while on the move. So together you can choose an activity. It may be as simple as standing while working or listening to music, or playing with a puzzle at the same time they are doing something else. Ironically this distraction will help him/her focus better in the long run.

- **Allow them to respond out-loud**

Writing is sheer torture for many of these kids. You will find that learning to express themselves through writing is a necessity. There are times, for instance that in doing math, these children may get stuck when they have to write down how they got to an answer that in their head they already know. To jump from the "math calculating" part of their brain, to the "put the answer down on paper", may seem like an impossible task. It's as though there is a wall between these two areas. In this case, the "seeing" then "saying" modality is their strength and the child should be encouraged to use the method that they are successful at in order to reinforce their abilities.

- **Use visual and auditory blinders**

We know that any movement or noise can act as distractions. As a teacher I always found that the use of study carrels (desks with 3 sides) cut down on visual distractions. In addition, headphones are a good tool to use to eliminate unnecessary auditory distractions.

- **Don't do everything in every book**

    You don't have to do every problem in every exercise in every book. Just because there may be seventeen problems on the work sheet, it doesn't mean the child needs to do all of them in order to master the concept. Some can do with much less practice. On the other hand, if your child is having difficulty with the concept, then they probably require the practice in addition to an adjustment in teaching strategies or the types of teaching materials being used. It would be helpful to consult with the learning specialist of your school for help in this area.

- **Give your child a checklist**

    Prepare a checklist of the work that needs to be covered for the day. This is a good practice for you as well, as it keeps you on schedule for what needs to be done and it provides a good structure for your child. It also acts as a natural reinforcement, i.e., they feel so much satisfaction knowing that they have successfully completed a task as they check it off the list.

- **Watch your teaching tempo and style**

  Over time you will learn to monitor and adjust your volume and intensity. We have a tendency at times to talk in a teaching voice, which is usually loud and forceful. If we listen to ourselves and to the expressions of our child as we are teaching, we will naturally adjust our pace and style in order to be most effective. If you already have a more low-key teaching style and have found yourself wishing for more exuberance, wish no more. You already inherently have the right demeanor needed for teaching your child.

- **Forget what others think**

  You will undoubtedly come in contact with others who will have their own opinions and judgements on how best a child should learn. They may think you are too much of a disciplinarian or you are too structured. Don't listen, forget it! You're the one who has taken the time and researched how your child learns best. They may be well intentioned, but have no understanding at all about what the individual needs of your child are. So, smile politely when their well-meaning comments are sometimes off base. Just remember your child is a gift, with a special destiny in store for them and you are there to ensure that they get there.

CHAPTER 7

Parents and Teachers
A Partnership for Success

Parents are Partners

Your School and You, A Partnership for Success

In forming a partnership with your school everyone should be working together to nurture positive communications and to maximize the educational and social growth of your child. The focus here is to know that all of the academic and behavior management programs are mutually supported between the school and home.

By being a "present parent", you are sending the message that you wish to partner with your school and are there to support your child in every way.

Included here is a framework on how to develop a beneficial relationship, a partnership of support, between home and school.

- Set meetings with your teacher to take place on a regular basis. These conferences can be pre-designated as either planning meetings or as information updates.

- It is easy for us to feel intimidated by our school. Avoid being defensive and avoid putting the teacher on the defense. Be aware of your frustrations, confusion and anger prior to going into the meeting. Address the issues in a positive tone to ensure the most beneficial results from the meeting.

- Most teachers and support personnel are eager to work with you. By going into the meeting with an attitude of respect, in most cases the response will be productive.

- Keep to topics that have to do with issues around your child and his/her academic, social or emotional issues.

- Let others see you as an advocate for your child. One that is persistent and fair. One that will not stop until they have achieved the best possible service for their child.

- If your child requires additional or supportive assistance, enlist the help of the head of the child study team to guide you in the direction of where best to find this service within the school system.

- Keep the school informed as to those extra curricular activities, which your child is involved in within the community.

- Keep the school informed as to any relevant issues, which may be happening at home (any changes in routine, major emotional upsets within the family etc.). This will help the teacher to better understand any sudden changes in the character of your child.

- Whenever possible, volunteer your time to help in the classroom or in some other area in the school (e.g., library, lunchroom). Get to know the school and let them get to know you as well. Your participation will send the message to your child and to the school, that you value their performances.

- Make requests in writing and keep copies of them on file for future reference. Follow up and be persistent in being given responses. Let them know that you mean business when it comes to the well being of your child.

- Gratitude goes a long way, so let the school know how grateful you are for their work and their interest in your child.

How to Prepare for Conferences

Parent/Teacher conferences should have a specific agenda, which results in an increased understanding of the child, how they are learning, and their performance in specific academic and social areas. You, as the parent, have the right, as well as the responsibility, to see to it that all of these areas are addressed at these meetings.

The following suggestions may help when you are preparing for the meeting:

- Beforehand, ask the teacher what is on their agenda and let them know the questions that will be asked of them and what it is you wish to accomplish from the meeting. This will provide a concise plan for what is to come out of your time together.

- Listen carefully to what the teacher is saying and take notes. If you don't understand something ask for clarification.

- Express your concerns about how your child is doing in school and share with them what is happening at home as well. Ask for the teachers' perspectives and give yours. Be open to help them or accept their help wherever possible.

- Stay involved. Monitor the progress of the child continuously. When your child does not seem to be responding to a particular teaching technique, meet with the teacher to discuss new methods or strategies. Request additional school support for your child whenever needed.

In practically all cases students are invited to these conferences. Encourage them to be involved in setting their own goals. Have them share their views and opinions of what their progress has been. Enlist their involvement and encourage them to be responsible for their own learning.

Building Academic Success

Many children labeled at-risk, are failing to thrive within our current school environments.

For children with ADHD, school very quickly becomes a challenging proposition, impacting every aspect of their life. The failure rates of an ADHD child are more than double that of other children. About fifty percent repeat a grade by the time they reach high school.

Thirty-five percent eventually drop out of school and only about five percent complete college. One study found that by age eleven, eighty percent were at least two years behind in reading, writing, spelling and math.

A long-term study found that forty-six percent of children with ADHD had been suspended and eleven percent had been expelled. Taken together, expulsion and dropout rates approach fifty percent, which is an alarming statistic, since children with ADHD compose up to seven percent of the population.

As previously discussed, the three main characteristics of ADHD are inattention, impulsivity and hyperactivity. Children with ADHD pay attention to what is novel or stimulating and have trouble focusing on the "important information". Their inability to sustain attention, especially during activities that require repetitions, is seen as misbehavior. Their impulsiveness causes difficulty in such tasks as, raising hands to answer questions, reading or listening to directions, and any activity that requires planning and organizing.

Traditional classroom practices are making schooling an absolute nightmare for many children with learning difficulties. Although wonderful in theory, the practice of inclusion (integration of exceptional children into mainstream learning environments) is just not working. The inherent lack of available individualized programming for these special needs children as well as the fact that there are not enough trained personnel to assist the teaching staff make the program a nightmare for those involved. From kindergarten on, the child's inability to inhibit their impulsive behavior prevents these kids from meeting the most simple of classroom demands for self-control and self-direction. Tasks like, staying in their seats until given permission, raising their hands before talking out, paying attention to authority figures, completing work that may have time limitations and staying organized are almost impossible for them to be successful with.

Some researchers feel that many home and school problems experienced by these children do not result solely from inborn, biological or genetic factors but from a mismatch between the child and the way that their learning environments are organized around them.

Research implies that success or failure depends on how we are seeing, planning and organizing our homes and schools in relationship to the individual child's particular demands. The question we ask ourselves is "Are our expectations both at home and at school in line with the needs and skill levels of our child"? "Are our programs focused and detailed enough to guarantee the success that this child so desperately needs"? "Do we possess the pre-requisites required to deal effectively with these children in a one to one, or small group level?"

School's Response to Academic Failure

Too often we are assuming that the child is the problem. This dangerous approach is isolating our child within the only learning and social environment that they know. Our parents and teachers are frustrated by the lack of resources, limited time, increasing stress levels and crowded classrooms. We have long ago come to the realization that unless we alter our learning environments and intervention strategies for our ADHD children, these negative outcomes will continue.

Sharing Responsibility for Learning

A Holistic Approach

In order to build academic success into our programming. A new vision of educational interventions is needed. One that considers the "whole child", and one that is based on a "complete wellness" paradigm. We need to be the facilitators for children and teach them that it is possible to change their attention and behavioral difficulties through discovering and working with their own strengths rather than attempting to put a band-aid on their faults. We must focus on the positive qualities of these children and what their inherent abilities could mean in contributing to their successes within the classroom, their homes and in society.

It has been my practice and experience that these children do better in activities that are hands on, and self-paced. Computers, tape recorders, and easels are powerful learning tools for them. The non-traditional teaching methods become the most effective ones. Our interventions must reflect the full sense of the child's true nature.

The treatment requires a combination of the academic, behavioral, nutritional, and medical modalities. For this to work it requires a partnership and shared responsibility between the parent, health care professionals and school personnel working together to design a program that addresses the individual child's weaknesses as well as builds on their strengths.

These interventions include, the need to further educate parents and teachers so that they may become more effective facilitators in regards to their child's academic, emotional and physical needs. When working in conjunction with the school, families can seek out information, training and counseling and can communicate and collaborate with the school and teachers to support their child. Schools can help to provide information and access to the school and its resources as well as providing individualized programming designed to meet the needs of the child in order to support the family.

Individual Modifications

Since no two children have the same strengths and weaknesses, specific modifications that compensate for individual weaknesses are critical to the success of children with learning challenges.

- Find the time when the child is most alert. Typically, mornings are better for focused work such as seatwork. Afternoons are best for more open-ended activities such as art, music, gym and group activities.

- Limit television and video games to one hour per day. Refrain from using these as a means of simply keeping the child occupied. Avoid any programming with a violent content.

- Place the student in a classroom with an understanding and flexible teacher who sets clear and consistent limits. This environment needs to be supportive and stress free so that the child feels emotionally safe to make mistakes. This will lead to better self-esteem and even add to their concentration and attention levels.

- Establish a daily communication system between teachers and parents. Allow for frequent telephone conversations between home and school so that everyone is informed of any changes. Encourage positive changes by writing notes to each other alluding to the positive as well as negative behavior of your child.

- Encourage the child to choose a mentor or confidant with whom problems may be discussed.

- Have your child seek out a friend who can help them with the work that they find more difficult. It could be a note taking, cafeteria, playground, or bus buddy.

- Allow the child opportunities throughout the day for additional physical activity. Take them to the park, arrange for an exercise program that perhaps the two of you can do together, give them little jobs around the house.

- Allow for the child who is easily distracted by outside noises to wear a headset when doing homework or working on assignments in the classroom. If the student wishes to listen to some music and works appropriately. Why not make the allowance.

- Recognize that the child is experiencing ongoing anxiety and fear about their academic and social performance. Although the student may understand that they have learning difficulties, they may need a place to safely release their high frustration levels.

- Provide the student with a place to go where they feel safe to express these emotions. This is not a time out and they should not see this as a punishment.

- Parents and teachers should meet to discuss solutions to socially inappropriate behaviors and be consistent in enforcing corrective measures.

Classroom Modifications

In planning for a successful learning experience for your child, it is important to know that there are modifications that can be made in your child's classroom to better meet their needs. When the Individual Education Plan (IEP) is being prepared you may wish to consider some of the following as recommendations:

- Teachers are required to set clear and explicit expectations of the child as a means of reducing the anxiety levels that the child may already be experiencing.

- Teachers should state the rules and repeat them often, showing patience and compassion.

- They should provide a structured routine and prepare the child for the transition times in their day.

- They should model respectful behavior. If the child is treated with respect he is more likely to manifest the same behavior with others.

- These students should be provided preferential seating in the classroom. A place where the child can be easily monitored and supervised. Surround the student with peers who can model appropriate behaviors for them to learn by.

- For some activities, study carrels can be used to eliminate stimuli.

- The classroom should have established learning centers that offer a variety of materials. This diversity helps maintain interest and provides some freedom of movement for the hyperactive child.

- The student should be taught how to maintain their notebooks and daily agenda.

- Have an extra supply of materials, such as papers and pencils available. Keep the supplies in a box labeled with the student's name.

- Wherever possible, keep an extra set of textbooks and supplies at home to alleviate the stress of the child forgetting them at school.

- The student may need to be shown how to take care of their materials and be allowed time during the day so they may organize themselves and their equipment. This practice should be repeated as often as necessary until the student gets into a good routine.

- The child should be allowed some additional time at the end of the day to get themselves prepared for departure. Go over with the child what they need to be taking with them in order to do the assigned homework.

Teaching Modification

- The teacher may wish to provide extra time for transition between activities and changes in classrooms.

- The teacher should be cognizant of sounds and noises that may be interfering with the child's ability to concentrate.

- Watch that the child is paying attention. Strategies for obtaining attention might include a verbal or nonverbal cue. Nonchalantly walking over and touching the child's desk or shoulder may be another method. This should be discussed beforehand with the child and they can help in choosing ways that will help in their refocusing of attention.

- Do not require eye contact from the child, this in itself may be distracting to the child and trigger varying degrees of discomfort.

- Make sure directions are given in a clear and concise way. Where possible, provide these directions both verbally and written. Demonstrations are an effective teaching method. A special buddy to be there as a coach is effective as well.

- Always have the student confirm their understanding by restating the directions or working through some examples.

- Always provide learning activities through which the child will experience success. Make sure that the work assigned is taught at the appropriate instructional level for the child.

- Homework should always be at the review level and be able to be done independently by the child.

- Determine whether the child feels capable and has the skills of performing the task at hand. Although as teachers and parents we are in the best position to know, often we are unaware that the student cannot do something and is unwilling to admit that some tasks are too difficult to complete.

- Find out where the child's level of frustration kicks in. Break assignments down into 10-minute segments. This may avoid the child becoming easily discouraged and overwhelmed when confronted with long assignments.

- Alternate seatwork with other kinds of learning activities by using learning centers. This type of structure can be developed at home as well. In addition, vary the presentation of materials making use of all available modalities, e.g., tape recorder (Auditory), television (Visual), blackboard/easel (Motor and Tactile).

- The use of games and hands on experiments allow children to touch, see, participate and create. Since they naturally love to work with their hands and actively participate, why not use this as a learning tool.

- Teach the child the necessary steps to complete a task. Record the steps on a flash card and make it accessible for the child to be able to look at it.

- Unfinished classroom assignments should not be sent home. If the child is not able to finish it in school, chances are they will not be able to complete it at home either. It creates confusion, conflict and power struggles between the child and yourself.

Anger/Behavior Management Techniques

- Arrange with the school for an effective behavior management plan. One that requires home as well as school participation.

- Provide the restless or anxious student with a squeeze toy (non-squeaking). This is a very effective way to vent frustration and it helps to focus the child. It is a great tool for all ages by helping with fine motor coordination and the strengthening of wrists and fingers.

- Encourage the student to first recognize and then verbalize feelings before losing control and if they do lose control, discuss with them the choices they have in order to bring themselves back into control.

- Never enter into a power struggle with the child, but learn to recognize the signs and to redirect the child's anger to something, which will provide either a safe place for them to vent or an activity that calms them down.

- Teach the child to recognize the signs their body shows them prior to their loosing control, e.g., feeling hot, quick heart beat, stomach pains, tension in muscles.

- Remain calm, avoid lecturing, and do not become engaged in arguments.

What we should know as a Parent – Academic Interventions

As your child's advocate it is important to know what the available services are, both within the community and those that may be provided by your school system. These specialists become valuable assets when you and your child's teacher require recommendations for day-to-day management.

The following specialists usually exist within every school board.

Child Support Team

This support team meets on a regular basis to consider the needs of children who are experiencing difficulties within the classroom. The team is usually made up of an administrator, a classroom teacher, a special education teacher, a psychologist and any other applicable support personnel. The purpose of the team is to brainstorm with the teacher and to develop strategies to help the child with their individual learning difficulties. The next step would be to refer the child for a psycho-educational evaluation if warranted.

Learning Disabilities and Resource Room Teacher

Both the Learning Disability Teacher and the Resource Room Teacher are trained to provide services to children who are experiencing academic problems. The classroom teacher may consult with the Learning Disabilities teacher to obtain strategies for accommodating the child's special learning needs within the course material. The resource room might be made available to a child who requires additional academic support. This room is a quiet place, which provides materials that are designed to address the specific academic weaknesses of the child. The room offers both small group and individual instruction and takes away the pressures of the regular classroom.

School Psychologist

The school psychologist is trained in the areas of assessment, academic instruction, counseling and classroom management. The school psychologist conducts psycho-educational evaluations to assess the intelligence, learning modalities, academic achievement and emotional functioning of children with learning and emotional difficulties. The information from these evaluations is used to develop an individual education plan designed to meet the specific needs of the child.

Speech and Language Therapist

The speech and language therapist evaluates and provides therapy for a child who is having difficulty processing or expressing language. This person is trained to mediate difficulties in the areas of articulation, auditory processing, verbal comprehension, expressive and receptive vocabulary development, word retrieval, sequencing, organization and the expression of language.

The speech and language person works in conjunction with the classroom and resource room teachers in the carrying out of program plans.

Neurologist

The neurologist is not found in the school system but may be recommended by them to evaluate any possible neurological disorder that may exist. The neurologist assesses fine and gross motor coordination, auditory and visual processing, sensory perceptions and recommends intervention strategies, which may include medication therapy.

Occupational Therapist

An occupational therapist evaluates and addresses problems affecting the motor and perceptual skills required for performing the activities of daily living and school functioning. These skills include correct posture, gross and fine motor coordination, visual perception and organization. The occupational therapist uses exercises and activities designed to address deficit areas found in the motoric functions. In addition, the occupational therapist provides equipment designed to develop handwriting and computer skills related to the school environment.

Individualized Education Plan (IEP)

If it is determined that your child is in need of special education and related services an IEP must be developed. This Individual Education plan must include the following components:

- Present level of educational performance for each subject area.

- Annual goals and short term objectives

- Specific educational services to be provided.

- Extent to which the child will participate in the regular classroom and resource room.

- Projected date for initiation and duration of services.

- The plan must include a method of determining whether the child is achieving the short-term objectives that have been set.

- Schedule and procedures for review.

This IEP must be decided upon in a meeting made up of an administrative representative of the school, the classroom teacher, the resource room teacher, any applicable support personnel (e.g., Speech & Language, psychologist, school counselor, occupational therapist) the parents and the student if appropriate. Either the parents or the school may have additional experts or consultants participate as well.

The Purpose and Functions of the IEP Process

- It serves as a communication vehicle between the school and the parent. It allows the participants to decide what the students needs are, what services will be provided and what the anticipated outcomes may be.

- It is a binding agreement which expresses a commitment of personnel and educational resources necessary to provide educational and related services based upon the individual needs of the child.

- These agreed services are to be administered in the least restrictive environment for that child.

- It serves as an evaluation tool to determine the extent of the child's progress and any adjustments that have to be made as the process unfolds.

Information Included on the IEP

The IEP should include the following pieces of information:

- Academic information.

- Academic achievement.

- Auditory and visual processing ability.

- Language ability (Both expressive and comprehension).

- Motor ability.

- Social Skills.

- Neurological functioning ability.

- Life skills ability.

In carrying out the responsibilities of the IEP, this committee goes through the following steps:

- Outlining areas of concern.

- Prioritizing long-term goals.

- Writing short-term objectives for these prioritized goals.

- Making a placement recommendation.

- Making specific recommendations how to implement the plan.

- Establishing criteria for the evaluation of all stated goals.

Outlining Areas of Concern

The first task is to review the information gathered by the evaluation process. This becomes the basis of the IEP. The committee should list the child's present levels of performance in each learning area, including both strengths and weaknesses and areas in need of intervention from support services.

Prioritizing Long-Term Goals (Annual Goals)

Decide which needs should be addressed first based on the following considerations:

- What are the priority parental concerns?

- What are the priority teacher concerns?

- What are the appropriate developmental sequences of tasks and behaviors that the child would be expected to move through?

- Identify behaviors that are inhibiting the child's ability to learn effectively?

For each of these priorities a long-term goal (annual goals) statement is written. These goals should be written in measurable terms so that they may be easily evaluated. They include a description of an expected educational or social outcome.

Writing Short Term Objectives

For each long-term objective, the committee will develop several short-term objectives. These are intermediate teaching steps between the student's current ability and the annual goal. There should be at least three short-term objectives for each annual goal. These statements are described in measurable terms and contain the level of mastery being worked toward, the professionals who are responsible for teaching the skill and when and how the student's progress toward mastery will be reviewed. Mastery means that the child will perform at a specific rate of success over a specified period of time.

Specifying Services needed

For each of the objectives, the committee will specify the type of service needed to meet that objective.

Services can include, Physical Therapy, Occupational Therapy, Speech Therapy, Adaptive Physical Education.

On the IEP, the following information regarding these special services should appear:

- Name of the service.

- Who will provide the service?

- Objectives of the service.

- Date of onset.

- Date of Review.

- How and what types of evaluation procedures will be used.

- How many hours per week the service is to be provided.

Specifying Persons Responsible

Within each service area, the committee should assign a specific person who will be responsible for seeing that the objectives are met. If there is no person from the school who has been assigned then a person from some other service area should take on that responsibility. For example, if the child needs speech therapy, but there is no speech therapist, then another implementers, e.g., the teacher should be assigned responsibility for planning and concentrating on extra language development activities.

Specifying Percentage of Time

For each service area, the committee will estimate a percentage of time that will reflect how much time the child will spend in receiving that particular service. For each objective, the committee should establish a time when services will start and services are expected to end. The committee will also set dates that it will review the child's progress towards the annual goals and short-term objectives.

Making a Placement Recommendation

The committee will also decide upon a placement recommendation. This placement should reflect the place in the school system where the services needed by the child, will best be delivered. It should also reflect the capabilities of the school system to deliver the special services.

Making Specific recommendations for Implementation

This committee may make specific suggestions to the service providers. Such suggestions may include types of activities to use in reaching the goals, resource material, and resource persons.

Establishing Objective Evaluation Criteria

For each goal statement, the committee should state how that goal would be evaluated. If the goals and objectives have been set in measurable terms then the criteria has already been set.

The evaluation procedures are to determine if satisfactory progress toward the annual goal is being achieved; if the goals and/or objectives need revision and how often that revision will happen; if and when services need to be altered and if and when the student can benefit from a least restrictive environment.

IEP Meeting Checklist for Parents

- Obtain school records, including all assessments, any past IEP's, report cards, teachers notes, progress notes.

- Make a list of your child's present levels of functioning, i.e. reading and math levels, academic strengths, dominant learning modalities, emotional strengths, behavioral and academic weaknesses.

- Make a list of academic, social and emotional goals that you have for your child.

- Make a list of additional services that you feel your child requires.

- Remember that you have an equal decision making role in this IEP process.

- If you feel it is needed, bring an advocate with you that you can consult with during the IEP meeting. Remember this is your child; be assertive and go for what you feel your child needs.

- If you disagree with the contents of the IEP you do not have to sign it and a follow up meeting may be required.

- Always get a copy of the IEP for your records.

- Monitor the course of your child's progress to insure that the goals are being carried out and the services are provided. Arrange for a schedule of meetings during the semester so if any adjustments need to be suggested or made they can be implemented.

- You can request a review of your child's IEP at any time during the school year[15].

CHAPTER 8

Overall Educational Requirements
The Curriculum

A curriculum that is irrelevant to a student's social and academic interests has been shown to contribute to poor performance, dropping out and rebellious behavior. To be motivating to any student, the curriculum needs to be applicable, interesting and provide opportunities for creativity. It goes without saying that offering children with ADHD meaningful learning experiences helps them to focus and concentrate.

To promote learning there should be active interaction and a sharing of information with other classmates. A curriculum should be designed that relates topics to the students' lives and concerns, one that involves the child through inquiry and hands-on experiences and one that teaches responsibility and problem-solving through real life applications.

Academic Interventions

Other than identifying what your child's strengths and weaknesses are and how they may be impacted by their learning styles, the next most important area to identify is what curriculum to use, and then to develop academic interventions around it so that your child will be receptive to the material being presented.

Many parents hesitate or may be embarrassed to ask their child's teacher questions, or they may be at a loss to know what questions to ask which would help them better understand the problems their child is having in school. As a layman it is easy to become confused. If your child is having a successful learning experience, you can assume that the school has found an effective way to teach your child. On the other hand if your child is not succeeding, either their teacher has not yet found a way to tap into your child's abilities, or they feel he/she lacks the ability to adapt to their methods of teaching.

The objective of any curriculum is to develop the most individualized learning program, based upon the specific needs of each child and to adapt teaching strategies based upon these individualized learning styles. Most teaching materials are designed to teach the Auditory, Visual and Kinesthetic learning styles. It has been found that students respond best when engaged in "hands on" learning activities. All programs should be designed to reflect the child's individual learning pace.

Most of the learning difficulties are diagnosed in reading, oral expression, written expression and math calculation. Practically any student is capable of learning when teaching strategies are modified to their level of functioning.

We assume that if a teacher has gone through the appropriate training that they should also be an authority in the teaching of reading, which is not always the case. The teaching of reading can be classified as an art form, which comes from experience and dedication to the subject area. If you are not satisfied with the method or way in which it is being taught, do not be intimidated. You owe it to yourself and more importantly to your child to investigate other avenues.

There are a variety of reading programs available. It becomes the responsibility of the educational professional to identify the program best suited to meet the individual needs of your child. Quite often this means using a combination of programs, which incorporate the visual, auditory and tactile modalities.

Sight Program - teaches reading through the development of sight or visual recognition.

Phonetic Program - teaches reading using both the visual and auditory modality

Whole Language Program - provides a language-rich environment, in which students explore connections among reading, thinking, writing, speaking and listening. The strategy emphasizes comprehension and interactive thinking.

Questions To Be Asking About Your Child's Reading Skills

- At what grade level is my child reading at?

- Can they answer questions directly related to the story?

- Can they locate specific information within the text of a story?

- Can they identify the main idea of the story?

- Can they draw conclusions from the story and then provide an explanation as to why they drew that conclusion?

- Can they follow written directions?

- Can they follow sequences?

- Can they make predictions?

- Can they determine inferences or "read between the lines?"

- Can they think critically about what they have read?

It has been discovered that some children cannot learn through any one particular sensory channel so a multi-sensory approach is used, employing the visual, auditory, kinesthetic and tactile senses.

An example of this procedure would be:

- A word is selected and written with marker or crayon on paper. Writing the word on sandpaper is most effective. The child then traces the word with finger contact, saying each part of the word as they trace it. The finger must be in contact with the paper to employ the use of the tactile senses. The process is repeated as often as it is necessary for them to learn to write the word.

- Give the child an opportunity to hear the word, see the word, feel the object and then write the word.

- Once the word has been written, have the student use it within a sentence.

- When the child is able to successfully use this new word in a sentence, have the child file the word in their "word file box". This helps to build their vocabulary.

- It is important that the child know the meaning, or different meanings, of all of the new words that they are learning.

- After continued repetition of these techniques, the child will develop the ability to simply be able to learn new words by looking at them sound them out, observing how the word is used in a sentence, and repeating them over to themselves.

Academic Interventions Used To Teach Reading To Children With Attention Difficulty

- To help reduce impulsivity, encourage your child to use their finger to track words as they read.

- Have the student mark any directions that are given with a highlighter.

- Evaluate reading skills, including the ability to decode words. Assess mastery of sight vocabulary and make adjustments where necessary.

- Determine whether the child can read better silently or out loud.

- Provide oral reading practice at a lower skill level to build confidence and fluidity of oral speech.

Reading Comprehension

- Provide remediation material that focuses on:

  - Following directions;
  - Using the context;
  - Locating the answer;
  - Getting the main idea; and
  - Drawing conclusions.

  There is an excellent remediation program put out by "Barnell Loft," that teaches all of the above skills.

- Encourage the child to organize information into categories. For example, names, dates and places are easier to remember if they are grouped together in small groups.

- Help the child to learn to visualize the information being read. Allow for them to create mental images and then let them talk about them. If possible allow them to write down or draw what these images are. Remember grammar is not as important at this stage, expression and exploration of creativity is.

- Encourage the child to listen to a tape or watch a video on the subject. This provides for the use of another modality to help the child comprehend the subject matter.

- Have the child write or tell a summary focusing on the who, what, where, when, why and how questions.

Written Comprehension

Written expression is a very complex skill and most children with reading difficulties find it a chore. It requires the integration of cognitive skills, sustained attention and efficient fine motor ability. The child must be able to plan, organize and sequence their ideas. The ADHD child has considerable difficulty expressing their ideas in writing.

The following are some interventions you may choose to use:

- Teach the child how to choose ideas for writing from materials that they have read, from movies, T.V., or experiences and trips that they have had.

- Teach the child how to make an outline.

- Teach the child how to organize their thoughts around the who, what, where, when, how and why questions.

- Reinforce with the child to use the computer as a writing tool. This reduces stress, as the computer will circumvent areas such as spelling, grammar and punctuation.

Mathematics

Frequently Asked Questions About Mathematics

- What grade level is my child functioning at?

- Inquire about having an additional textbook at home.

- What is my child's ability to do mental computation?

- What is my child's ability to do one-step and two-step word problems in math?

- What concepts are covered in this math program?

- How will I know when my child masters a concept?

Other Subjects

Frequently Asked Questions About Social Studies, Physical Science, Health

- What specific units have been covered?

- What skills has my child learned through these studies?

- Does my child know how to summarize and outline course material?

- Do they know how to make charts, mapping, note taking, study skills, test preparation skills, research project skills, finding reference books for study/research and time management skills.

In summary, you may want to carry these questions with you and seek some answers from your school when it comes to the planning of your child's education plan:

- Does the teaching strategies draw on your child's strengths or does it focus on their weaknesses?

- Does the curriculum interest, challenge and engage your child?

- Is the curriculum relevant to your child's academic and social needs?

- Are the assessment techniques measuring what your child really knows?

- Does your school provide accommodations that will allow for your ADHD child to be successful?

- Does your classroom teacher have and take the time to meet with you, collaborate with peers, and spend time as required with your child?

We cannot afford to let at-risk children, including those with ADHD, fail in school. Failure deprives them from being productive members of their community. As advocates for our children we must take a hard look at how we can reach and teach these children. We must use every bit of experience and piece of information at hand to ensure that they are successful in their academic and social endeavors.

Educational Strategies

The following information is organized around the five main areas of learning as used by our educational system to identify children with learning deficiencies.

This information will help you in three ways:

- It will give you several strategies to work with at home.

- It will identify the specialist that can help you with the specific area of difficulty that your child is having.

- You will be more knowledgeable when discussing educational strategies with the teacher and school learning team.

Oral Expression
(Speech & Language Therapist)

- Teach your child breathing techniques (see chapter on exercise), this will help to slow speech patterns, calm them down, and help your child organize their thoughts before speaking.

- Teach your child to let the listener know what the topic of discussion is and when they are changing topics.

- Reinforce the use of complete sentences using who, what, when, where, how and why.

- Let your child know that it is OK to be misunderstood, that it is very common and that it happens to you as well. Get them into the habit of restating the information in a more clear and concise way.

- Use pictures to teach your child how to tell a story.

- Determine whether your child can identify their feelings, articulate and understand them.

- Use a tape recorder or videotape as a teaching tool, to show areas of weakness or strength. Videotape yourself to show your child that there are areas you can improve on as well.

Listening Comprehension
(Learning Specialist, Speech & Language)

- Make sure that your child understands the level of vocabulary that is being used by you and their teacher.

- Use a combination of verbal, visual and tactile cues to aid in communication.

- Use single step instructions and then add on to these, based upon the child's level of comprehension.

- Present oral directions in small concrete steps with a pause between each step and check for level of understanding.

- When necessary repeat directions.

- Have your child repeat or write down the directions for you and then you can give confirmation or restate your meaning for further clarity.

- Try not to show frustrations. Compassion, patience and understanding on your part allows more space for your child to learn through trial and error.

Basic Reading Skills
(Reading Specialist/Speech & Language)

Reading is a very complex skill to learn. I have often thought that learning how to read is truly one of those miracles that we rarely think about. Actually, like anything else, it is a process and if you follow a step-by-step procedure you will find that it will culminate with success.

- Encourage your child to use their finger to help them with difficulties in losing their place, skipping lines or omitting words.

- When necessary, have your child use headphones to block out any auditory distractions.

- Allow your child to read in whatever comfortable position they may choose.

- Use pictures to teach letter-sound combinations.

- "Glass Analysis" is a very effective reading program that teaches reading through phonetics and decoding.

- Determine whether your child can read better silently or orally.

Reading Comprehension

- There is an excellent remedial program put out by "Barnell Loft" that helps support reading comprehension.

- Have your child read the comprehension questions before beginning to read the passage so that they can recognize the answers as they come across them.

- Keep the stories short.

- Use stories that are of high interest.

- If the child is more comfortable moving around while reading allow them to do so.

- Make your directions clear and concise.

- Take into account your child may have difficulty with memory, so do not expect mastery too soon after teaching a new skill. Provide repetition and drill to ensure mastery. Mastery is defined as knowing a set of information 90 percent of the time over an extended period of time. (e.g. 9 out of 10 correct for 6 consecutive days) You must acquire mastery before moving on to the next skill.

- Present only a limited amount of information so that your child is able to store and retain it.

- To help with memory, teach your child to associate information with personal life experiences or to use mnemonic deices, e.g., the lines in the treble clef music staff would be - E, G, B, D, F – Every Good Boy Deserves Fudge.

- Have your child read out loud as much as possible and reading out loud to them is very effective as well.

- Have your child act out or role play the stories they are reading.

- Wherever possible, make use of recorded books.

- Keep vocabulary lists.

Handwriting

The majority of Learning Disabled, Attention Deficit Hyperactive Disorder, Obsessive Compulsive Disorder (OCD) and Tourette syndrome children have handwriting problems. The ADHD child is impulsive, writes very quickly and in a disorganized style. When the child is encouraged to finish in a timely manner, both the legibility and content are affected. The Tourette child may have hand and arm tics that affect their handwriting. The OCD child may feel the compulsion to write and rewrite words and erase until there is a hole in the paper. Because of these problems work is not completed. The child becomes frustrated and very often refuses to do any writing at all.

The following are some recommendations:

- Permit your child to use a computer.

- Keep handwriting work to a minimum.

- Help your child by writing what your child dictates to you.

- Allow your child to choose either manuscript or cursive writing, depending on which is easier and produces the best results.

- Instead of writing answers on paper, permit your child to record into a tape recorder.

- Have their teacher assign a "note-taking buddy" to assist them.

The Use of Computers as a Teaching Tool

With the ongoing evolution of the personal computer there has come a "learning revolution" in which both parents and educators agree that this interactive resource makes learning fun. This tool has changed the way we view educational development and learning.

The computer is a combination of graphics, sound, video and music. It is a smorgasbord of things that appeal to both children and adults. Software has been formatted to be used for every corner of our educational environment, for every subject area, for every level of academic and social performance. It has been designed to attract the two-year-old, the ninety-two year old, the gifted, the developmentally disabled, the hyperactive child and the child who has Attention Deficit Disorder. It is a teacher, an educator, a bank of information and a place where we are constantly creating new information. It is a wonderful tool to reinforce what we have done and look back on our successes.

If presented in the right way, the child will learn more with the use of a computer than during an equivalent amount of time with traditional teaching methods. It is a well-known fact that we learn better and faster when the material used to teach us is FUN! The combined use of the visual, auditory and tactile modalities enhance learning material and retention, especially with children who have special needs. Computers in a way, offer us an alternative way to improve on the way we educate our next generation of children.

After saying all of this, it must not be forgotten that computers are just a tool. It is no surprise that this technology has affected our lives to a great extent. For those of us who adapt to change well, our lives will be richer for this growth and our children will develop similar attitudes and motivations. Computers are only a small part of this bigger picture. As the use of computers becomes more common within the home environment, parents are realizing how quickly their children are learning and retaining information with the use of this tool.

Reasons for the Use of Computers

- It helps to build self-esteem and is a good motivator especially for the underachiever.

- It helps to introduce new concepts and develop research and writing skills.

- It is a great reinforcement and helps to increase interest in learning. It also helps to develop creativity.

- Computers are the perfect supplement and tutor for the learning challenged child. This includes those with

ADHD, Dyslexia, Apraxia, Developmental Disabilities and learning Disabilities. It allows for the child to move at their own pace and their own academic level.

Access to computers and proficiency in their use are not luxuries any longer. They have become pre-requisites for learning and optimizing productivity. More and more families and schools are using computers as a tool for tutoring. Curriculum software has been developed to include the "core" subject areas such as reading, writing, math, social studies and social skills.

The Computers as a Teaching Device

Studies consistently show that children absorb more when the information is presented both visually and auditorily and the computer is playing an increasingly larger role both at home and in the classroom. It is generally acknowledged that children learn quickly when they are introduced to computers. Much of this depends on the age of the child, the amount of parental involvement/supervision and the type of programs which are used. The type of software should be based on the child's age, interests and developmental level. Younger children (2-7 yrs.) require programs that have high content of graphical and auditory mix especially where reading and writing are concerned. The cartoon-like movement on the screen captivates them. The older child (8-15 yrs.) requires less supervision and graphical programs, with more of an emphasis on programs that keep daily records and track progress. These programs allow for you to evaluate their mastery of skills, concepts and how they are applying them.

Computers and the Special Child

Through the use of computers, the ability of children to retain what is perceived, processed and learned is accomplished more quickly when the multi-media format is employed. With these children, this visual, auditory and tactile tool becomes an even more useful method for teaching since so many of them have trouble with directing their attention and with memorizing directions. Those teachers and parents that I have talked to, report that students learn more, pick-up concepts faster and enjoy learning more then those students who do not have access to this learning tool.

Concerns about the use of Computers

There are some concerns or misconceptions regarding the use of computers as educational tools:

- One concern of parents is that the computer will take away from parental time or interaction with their child. There is some truth to this, however, if the right curriculum is chosen you can use this time to explore and structure more educational training. Supervision is important because you do not want the child to just use the computer to play games. So like anything else, you set limits of what can and can't be done.

- The computer intimidates some parents. The more you play with it the easier it will become. We have all had to learn how to use this tool. Once familiarity kicks in, you will wonder how you ever lived without it.

- Some parents are concerned that if their children use the computer too much that they will be less interested in using books or in reading them. Through experience I have learned that the exact opposite is true.

Problem Areas Addressed

Attention - Children focus better and they are excited by the appeal of something that is interactive and fun. The computer allows the child to feel that they are in control, there is no one that may be standing over their shoulder to peer or judge them. This allows for a greater sense of confidence.

Impulsiveness – Again, the computer is a machine which is very forgiving and doesn't care how often you perform a task in order to master a task.

Study Skills - For the child who has difficulty with sequencing, the computer has a built-in structure which guides the child through various functions. Computer programs such as spelling and grammar check help with word skills. Computer games provide practice in logic, reasoning and sequencing. There are also programs that create databases, spreadsheets, and graphs.

Fine Motor Skills - It has been established that the majority of individuals with ADHD have significant difficulty with their handwriting skills. The use of a computer allows for the child to present work that is visually acceptable, thereby reinforcing their self-esteem.

Memory - The main focus of the computer is to be able to store and retrieve information. This becomes an invaluable tool for those individuals with memory problems.

Self-esteem - Productivity and performance at school form the basis of many decisions students make about their own self-worth. It is imperative that they be given every opportunity to succeed. Computer technology represents one of those tools that help to promote this healthy self-esteem. .

CHAPTER 9

What Does Proper Nutrition Have to Do With It?

As we continue to look at the entire picture of Exceptionalities, the following research will substantiate the remarkable impact that a good nutritional regime and vitamin/mineral supplements, have on various learning disabilities such as Dyslexia, Dyspraxia and ADHD.

You Are What You Eat

While the rate of Learning Disabilities and ADHD have more than tripled in North America during the past thirty years, it is interesting to note that there was a considerably lower incidence of any increase in European children and was almost non-existent in Japan. Yet, children of these descents who were raised in North America were affected at the same rate as native North American children.

I recently had the opportunity to spend time in India and while there I interviewed Pediatricians and Holistic Practitioners. It is completely uncommon for a child in this culture to be colicky or to come down with what we here in North America would consider normal childhood illnesses. Children there, rarely have tummy aches, rashes or ear infections, unlike the children raised here in North America, who experience them chronically. Not only do children of that culture enjoy better health, but the term ADHD is relatively unheard of. The exact opposite is certainly true here. Why is it so rare, for a North American child to enjoy continuous good health?

Chronic Undernourishment

Chronic undernourishment does not necessarily mean not getting enough food. The nutritional value within the foods we eat plays the most important role in our overall well being.

Consider the way in which our fruits and vegetables are farmed these days. There are very few farmers that are not in the practice of using pesticides for insect control and chemicals to stimulate the growth and color of the products they grow.

Now take a look at how livestock is being raised. They are force fed diets consisting mainly of carbohydrates to fatten them up for quicker sale, not to mention the vast amounts of antibiotics that are given to ensure they don't become diseased. Even farmed fish tend to contain less of the nutrients they did just a few short years ago because of the food that they are being fed.

Our diet has drastically changed over the last three decades, from foods rich in EFA's (Essential Fatty Acids. see pp.204) such as fish, green leafy vegetables and nuts to eating huge amounts of french-fries, doughnuts and potato chips (a personal favorite of mine) and other processed foods which are being prepared using solid fats. As we have been reducing our intake of EFA's, not only have we been depriving our brain of the nutrients it needs in order to function at its fullest potential, but we have also been increasing our risk of cardiovascular disease, diabetes and cancer. Because our digestive system isn't equipped to efficiently break down or use these fats, some of it is released into our system. As the fats travel through our system, they attach to the walls of our arteries and cells. Like a vehicle that has run for 100,000 km without having an oil change, our bodies get sluggish, perform terribly or breakdown altogether. Messages to the brain are scrambled and nothing works efficiently any longer.

Factor together the time constraints the modern family is under for meal preparation and that the food that we eat is becoming harder for our bodies to process and less beneficial to our overall health and you've got a recipe for disaster.

That old adage "you are what you eat" takes on a whole new meaning. Face it, we are consuming foods that are over processed and lacking in nutritional vitality.

Unhealthy nutritional regimes may be the main cause, and are at least a contributing factor to the following conditions:

- Hyperactivity
- Irritability
- Poor attention and ability to focus
- Fatigue
- Headaches
- Persistent colds
- Allergies
- Constipation/Diarrhea, bedwetting
- Poor school performance

Dr. Alan Gaby, a holistic medical doctor in Baltimore, Maryland calls it, "chronic sub-clinical everything syndrome". Everyone seems to be saying the same thing that they don't feel well, but their doctors cannot find anything clinically wrong with them. They go away feeling like hypochondriacs but still knowing that something just isn't right. Does this ring a bell?

Dr. Gaby believes that physicians, researchers and scientists aren't looking deep enough. He theorizes that people are undernourished and that the body is trying to tell us that it needs some help when we experience these feelings of being ill. Undernourishment can, and does, cause food allergies, cold and flu like symptoms, ear infections, ADHD and many other conditions, which are created by a suppressed immune system.

Essential Fatty Acids
Good Fats vs. Bad Fats

Essential Fatty Acids (EFA's) are a vital brain nutrient (our brain is comprised of 60% fats) without which, perception, cognition, memory and attention span wouldn't work properly.

The "essential" in essential fatty acids means that while it is essential that your body gets these Omega 3 or Omega 6 fatty acids in order to function properly, it is not something that the body is able to produce on its own. You supply it to your body through your nutritional intake. These fatty acids (EFA's) exist as a major component for the healthy functioning and development of the brain. It has been found that these EFA's are the building blocks of important membranes around and within nerve cells. For the brain to function properly it is a necessity that it receives the nutritional support of these EFA's.

Essential Fatty Acids have been found to be as important to your physical health as vitamins, proteins and carbohydrates. Like vitamins, the body cannot produce them on its own and they have to come from the food we eat. It is found in seed oils such as sunflower, safflower, corn, flaxseed and sesame. It is also found in dark leafy vegetables and some fish.

Dr. Jacqueline Stordy, author of the book *The LCP Solution* tells a story of how an Inuit mother unwittingly found a solution to her daughter's Dyslexic condition.

Mother and child had moved away from their native culture when the child was an infant. For a good part of the child's early life she was fed a diet that resembled that of the average North American child. During this time she exhibited all of the symptoms of a child that had Dyslexia. When the child had the opportunity to return to her homeland and began eating the diet of her culture which consisted mainly of the meat and fat of fish, whales and seals, her Dyslexia symptoms disappeared. It wasn't until this child returned to her old lifestyle that a correlation was made between the diet of the child and how it affected her Dyslexia.

Learning Disorders and Our Genes

Research supports that there is a common genetic basis to ADHD, Dyslexia and Dyspraxia as all of these conditions tend to have similar symptoms and can overlap traits of one another. In addition, the studies conducted so far strongly suggest a correlation with ADHD and a defect in fatty acid metabolism and that these learning disorders can be improved when an individual is supplemented with EFA's. Interestingly enough studies conclude that with the decrease in EFA's in our diet has come a dramatic increase in learning disorders.

The Immune System (Digestive and Brain Implications)

The following information reviews some of the latest research findings with regards to how nutrients affect the six organ systems that are involved in ADHD. These are the brain, the digestive system, the immune system, the skin, blood sugars and the blood itself. The information strongly suggests our need for changes in our nutrition.

The ADHD research being done today is providing insights on how the immune system is involved in creating ADHD symptoms. Research has shown that hyperactive children get more frequent head colds and have more allergies than most other children.

Eating sugar in any form, whether it is glucose, fructose, sucrose, honey, molasses, and fruit juice reduces the immune systems ability to function. This suppression of immune function can start within 30 minutes of ingestion and last for several hours.

Having the digestive system do its job is crucial to the functioning of the immune system. The digestive tract is an "early defense" for the immune system. In order to run efficiently, an immune system requires supplies of folate, biotin, vitamins A, D, B(6), B(12), zinc, iron, and essential fatty acids. All of these nutrients are absorbed through the digestive system.

Follow-up studies of children who have been diagnosed as having ADHD show that a considerable number do not have the ability to absorb various nutrients from their digestive tract. This creates a suppressed immune system and an opportunity for an increase of allergies.

A nonprofit nutrition advocacy group, The Center for Science in the Public Interest (CSPI), addressed the issue of diet and ADHD. The center has reported that 17 out of 23 double blind studies had found significant evidence that children's behaviors worsen after they consume artificial colors or certain foods such as milk or wheat products. One study found that children who suffer from allergies such as asthma or eczema improved with the addition of the EFA's in their diet. This is because an EFA deficiency makes the lining of the skin, lungs and stomach easier to be penetrated by materials that do not normally enter the body. The immune system reacts to this foreign matter as if it were antibodies that were invading the body. Histamine is released, bringing on cold/flu like symptoms, reddening and swelling in the form of skin rashes, sinus infections, ear infections or asthma. When the EFA's or LCP supplements are given, the lining tissues become less permeable and the individual then has fewer allergic reactions to the foods that cause the reactions. In its report, CSPI urged parents to consider modifying their children's diet as one of the alternatives to treating learning disabilities before resorting to stimulant drugs

The most important question for individuals with ADHD, Dyslexia and Dyspraxia is, "Do these supplements work"? Research positively supports these results. We know that the combination of fish oil together with Gamma Linoleic Acid is effective in relieving many of the characteristics of these disabilities. The next question is then, will these work for everyone. The answer is no. Dyslexia, ADHD and other learning disabilities may also be caused by brain injury from trauma, lack of oxygen at birth or trauma experienced in an accident. In these cases, a change in the nutritional program may be totally ineffective.

Allergy-based symptoms among children with ADHD are so common and so well researched that it is now possible to devise a list of the foods to which children and adults with ADHD are most likely to be allergic to. Milk, wheat, corn, yeast, nuts, citrus, chocolate, eggs, soy, beef and pork are the more commonly known ones.

At this point you have nothing to lose and everything to gain to have your child tested for food allergies and make the necessary adjustments in your child's diet.

The Digestive System

A healthy, well functioning digestive system will produce the following results:

- Complete breakdown of foods into their smallest components.

- Rich population of body-friendly bacteria and minimal growth of body-unfriendly bacteria.

- Intact interior lining and walls of the intestines.

- Timely, smooth processing of foods.

- Two to three healthy bowel movements per day.

Children who have ADHD are at risk for unbalanced performance of all of these functions.

Bacteria

One of the most important components for healthy absorption of foods into our system and the prevention of food allergies is a bacteria called, "Lactobacillus Acidophilus & Bifidus Bacterium".

This bacteria occupies the intestine by the billions and assists in the following:

- Creating lactase to digest milk sugars.

- Replenishing good bacteria.

- Producing Vitamin K and Vitamin B.

- Cleaning out the intestines of harmful toxins.

- Keeping your cholesterol at the correct level.

- It is Nature's natural deodorant.

- Aids in the production of enzymes.

- Helps reduce gas.

- Cleaning and beautifying the skin.

- Adds shine to your hair.

Most children with ADHD do not have enough good bacteria being produced in their system. The bottom line is these children are functioning with an inefficient digestive system, which leads to allergies, upset stomachs and constipation.

How to Improve Your Digestive System

Good habits include:

- Chewing foods well.

- Drinking liquids 30 minutes before or after a meal, rather than during.

- Eating fruit 30-60 minutes before a meal.

- Avoiding all food to which the child is allergic.

- Avoiding aspirin.

- Consuming freshwater blue-green algae; lecithin; foods rich in vitamin C; foods rich in essential fatty acids; or taking digestive enzyme supplements.

- Consuming vegetables that are fresh and raw or minimally cooked.

- Avoiding large amounts of sugar.

- Consuming a half-gallon of pure, bacteria free, chlorine free water daily.

Studies on Special Dietary Concerns

Food additives can profoundly affect a child's health and performance. In a New York City School study, 800,000 children were fed breakfast and lunch containing no sugar, color, additives or preservatives for five years. As a result of these dietary adjustments, their test scores improved by 42 percent.

Dr. Ben Feingold first discovered a connection between certain foods, food additives and children's behavior over 20 years ago. After studying over 1200 cases, Feingold concluded that 40-50 percent of hyperactive children are sensitive to artificial food colors, flavors and preservatives as well as foods containing salicylates. It is agreed by Pediatricians and Holistic Health Practitioners that sugar suppresses the immune system and has strong mood-altering effects.

Author Kharta Khalsa, met a three-year-old girl who had been diagnosed as disabled and was on her way to a special education class. When tested she had 35 food allergies, including the usual wheat, milk and corn. Although she had never been on antibiotics in her life, she was constantly fighting ear infections, which were barely controlled with herbal medicines. When her parents removed all allergic foods, her ear infections ceased. Even one corn chip, would cause a runny nose. So the parents supported this child's immune system with proper diet and nutritional supplements and within a year she became a candidate for the gifted program.

Another child who was found to be allergic to wheat products, had become so wild by the age of three that it was impossible to carry on a conversation while he was in the room. Within sixty days of having all wheat products removed from his diet he became relaxed, had an increased attention span, and was more focused. It was as if some magic had taken place for this little being and this child who was once diagnosed as hyperactive was transformed.

Unhealthy foods our body learns to ask for

- ADHD children crave salty or highly seasoned foods. The reason is that they are looking to satisfy the deficiencies of minerals in their bodies.

- They also crave cheese and other dairy products because their bodies are lacking in proteins.

- The number one most craved food is sugar. The theory is that their brains are not receiving enough of blood sugars as fuels so the body will naturally search for additional energy. The body is not prepared to receive all of this additional sugar in its bloodstream so, instead, insulin is sent into the bloodstream to keep blood sugar levels in balance. Doesn't this sound as bad as it really is for the body? The irony is that the brain never does get that increased fuel that it is demanding. What it does do is create an addiction for more sugar.

The best way to respond to these common demands from our bodies is to make available those foods and supplements that are rich in minerals and proteins. These will knockout these destructive sugar cravings.

Understanding Specific Nutrient Deficiencies

The benefits of protein

- Regulates blood sugar.

- Nurtures the brain cells.

- Creates stamina and energy.

- Builds healthy cells.

- Develops muscle tissue.

- Keeps our hormones in check.

- Helps to balance cholesterol.

- Provides a boost to the immune system.

- Builds healthy bone structures.

- Keeps our hair and skin healthy.

The billions of cells which make up our bodies all depend on protein to perform their functions, to make repairs, and to build new cells to replace old, damaged and worn out tissues. An inadequate supply of protein can lead to severe physical and emotional problems.

An excellent source of protein comes from Soy. It contains all the necessary amino acids. Amino acids are the building blocks of protein. There is considerable scientific evidence showing that soy is not only a superior source of protein, but it also contains natural compounds that provide a variety of health benefits. Studies done at the Mayo Clinic, Harvard, Duke and the University of

Illinois have revealed evidence of the performance of soy protein.

Their findings have shown the following health benefits:

- It promotes the development of Antioxidants, which protect cells from "free radicals", thus helping to prevent cancer
- Cholesterol can be reduced.
- Osteoporosis occurs less often.
- Helps to strengthen the immune system.

Benefits of B-Complex vitamins in our diet

If the B-Complex vitamin supply is inadequate it may cause the following symptoms:

- Irritability and/or hyperactivity.
- Nervousness and/or insomnia.
- Depression and wide mood swings.
- Fatigue.
- Anxiety.
- Low blood sugar.
- Headaches.
- Food and Alcohol cravings.

Benefits of Calcium/Magnesium in our diet

Helps to alleviate:

- Nervousness.
- Hyperactivity.
- Muscle aches and cramps.
- Joint pain.
- Tooth decay.
- Insomnia.
- Headaches.

It has been shown that 90% of us are low in calcium.

Benefits of Lecithin

- Effects brain and nerve tissue.
- Memory.
- Concentration.
- Skin.

Benefits of Vitamin C

- Immune system booster.
- It is a natural antibiotic.
- It is a natural antihistamine.
- Builds healthy skin.
- It is a stress fighter.

- Fights infection.
- Builds strong bones and cartilage.

Benefits of Zinc

- A deficiency will lead to abnormal fatigue.
- Can experience skin problems.
- Poor appetite.
- Lowered resistance.

Benefits of Iron

- A deficiency can lead to Anemia.
- Impaired concentration.
- Impaired memory and possible learning disabilities.

Benefits of GLA (Gamma Linoleic Acid)

Lack of GLA can lead to:

- Hyperactivity.
- Learning Disabilities.
- Asthma.
- Related skin problems.

Why Supplement your Diet?

Studies show that the average person experiences stress in some form, on the average of every ten minutes throughout the day.

Stress depletes B vitamins and vitamin C. These nutrients are critical to help us get the energy we need from our food and to keep our immune systems strong and healthy.

Stress also causes muscles to tighten up increasing our need for Calcium and Magnesium, which help muscles relax. Blood sugar rises too high and drops too low when our diets include excessive amounts of sugar, caffeine and processed foods. When our blood sugar drops too low, we experience fatigue, irritability, headaches and food cravings. The best way to stabilize our blood sugar is to take in adequate amounts of protein, fiber and B vitamins.

When looking for a good supplement you may want to look for one that is based on whole foods. These should consist of natural ingredients with no chemicals or additives and ones that are flavored with all natural sweeteners.

Nutritional Supplements

The supplement most widely used to ensure a proper daily dose of EFA's has been a fish oil-based capsule called Efalex. It contains evening primrose oil, vitamin E and thyme oil. Research indicates that these antioxidants help protect the fatty acids in the body and aid the fatty acids absorption into the body.

Some other supplements that can be taken to enhance one's diet and create a healthier nutritional environment are:

Juice + Gummies – provides natural fruit and vegetable powders, fruit and vegetable fibers and food enzymes, along with food actives and acidophilus. This product supplies your child the nutrition from 17 different fruits, vegetables and grains. It contains apples, oranges, pineapples, cranberries, peaches, acerola cherries and papaya. The vegetables include carrots, spinach, broccoli, kale, parsley, beets and tomato. It has grains such as barley and oats. All of these combine to provide a variety of nutrients that only "whole foods" offer. Imagine your child supplementing their diets with this and asking for more.

Pycnogenol - (Pine Bark extract) – This product has become widely known as one of the most powerful antioxidants available. It is often recommended by Nutritionists and Homeopathic Practitioners to reduce hyperactivity and increase the Child's ability to concentrate and focus. In some cases it is recommended as an alternative to Ritalin.

Perfect Food - Perfect food is a completely absorbable, highly concentrated whole food. Its vitamins, minerals, enzymes, essential fatty acids, amino acids and antioxidants are all from certified organic whole food. It contains Kamut Grass Juice, Barley Grass Juice, Alfalfa Grass Juice, Oat Grass Juice, Spirulina, Chlorella, Spinach Broccoli, Broccoli Sprouts, Kale, Cauliflower, Parsley, Dandelion Grass, Sea Kelp, Sea Dulse, and Sea Vegetables, Chia Seed, Flax Seed and ionic trace minerals. Each serving of perfect food is the nutritional equivalent of 10 servings of vegetables and 2 servings of fruit and can be taken as a meal replacement.

PURE SYNERGY - Pure Synergy is an alkaline blend made from certified organic ingredients with no bulk fillers. Superior Chinese Asian mushrooms and Western herbs are combined with organic grass juices, algae and sea vegetables. The combination of 11 different algae's and sea vegetables provides immune boosting. These herbs are freeze-dried so they retain their oils and healing ingredients. It is reported that Pure Synergy helps to stimulate mental clarity and offers ongoing defenses against stress and illness and furnishes deep nourishment for healing.

NEUROMINS – A number of clinical trials have been conducted using micro-algae. Most of the research has been focused on dietary needs of newborns for healthy brain and visual development. The ingredients include sunflower oil, Vitamin C, mixed carotenoids, Vitamin E. They are available in health food stores under various brand names such as, Natures' Way, Solgar, Solaray, Tree of Life.

ATTENTION! BARS – This is an ideal alternative for children who do not like to swallow pills. It contains a wealth of nutrients including fish oil. The taste is enhanced by chocolate peanut butter or very berry crunch flavoring[21].

GOLD CIRCLE FARMS – A Colorado company called Omega Tech, is producing eggs, which are highly enriched. They use marine algae, which is fermented and harvested and incorporated into the feed given to their hens.

NUTRI-KIDS SCHOOL AID- This is a vanilla flavored shake which mixes with milk or water and delivers carbohydrates, proteins in addition to many vitamins and minerals. The source of DHA is the Neuromins micro algae.

LACTOBACILLUS ACIDOPHILUS – This amazing little thing helps with the digestive process. Your child can take one or two with each meal and you can get this at your local health food store. The best types are those that are refrigerated.

Blue-Green Algae as a Dietary Supplement

Dr. Karl Abrams, a chemistry professor at Saddleback College in Southern California has done experimentation with "nutritional Blue-Green Algae". He personally experienced a greater sense of mental clarity, a boost in energy and an elevated feeling of well being. He has been acclaimed for his book entitled, "*Algae to the Rescue! Everything you need to know about Nutritional Blue-Green Algae*".

His research has been on the effects that algae has on children with ADHD. He found that the Blue-Green Algae could improve focusing abilities and attention spans in ADHD children.

A study using Blue-Green Algae done in Nicaragua revealed an increase in the academic scores of 1482 children who took just 1 gram of Blue-Green Algae daily. On the average academic scores went up by 17% in one year.

One particular study of blue-green algae involving 109 ADHD, nine-year-old children (55 girls and 54 boys) from across the United States. Parents filled out a detailed questionnaire that inquired about academic, medical and behavioral histories of their children. At the end of the ten-week study in which these children were supplemented with Blue-Green Algae, parents once again filled out another questionnaire and reported significant improvement in the child's ability to focus, follow directions and concentrate. They indicated that there were fewer symptoms of anxiety and depression and acting out behaviors. Teachers involved in the study also observed an improvement in the ability of the children to focus and also a reduction in aggressive and acting-out behaviors.

Other Dietary Supplement Studies

Studies on dietary alterations have shown dramatic effects both on physical health and mental functioning.

Michael and Lesley Colgan at the Colgan Institute of Nutritional Science in San Diego conducted a twenty-two week dietary study on children. They observed dramatic improvements in the learning abilities of 16 children diagnosed as having learning and/or behavioral problems. Their diets consisted of fiber, whole grains, unprocessed foods with no refined sugars, supplemented with a multi-vitamin/mineral supplement.

Another study found that vitamin and mineral supplementation could significantly increase non-verbal intellect in children. Vitamins such as thiamin, niacin and vitamin B-6 and B-12 are important to brain and nerve functioning.

Dietary Planning

As a parent, one of the most important responsibilities you have to your child and to the family as a whole, is to consider a complete nutritional program. Consideration should be given not only to a healthy menu, but also a considerable amount of thought and research into the supplements, which may be required.

You can improve the conversion of EFA's into the effective LCP's by avoiding foods that contain hydrogenated fats. This means becoming a smarter consumer. Checking out labels, avoiding margarine and cutting down on such foods as ice cream, chocolate, cookies, pastries, and potato chips. All foods that we all love and find it extremely difficult to resist. This may well be a daily struggle but one that will pay off for the entire family. Chances are that once your children are introduced to healthy eating, they will continue to eat in a healthy manner when they are adults as well.

There is considerable evidence that supports the theory that nutritional supplements are beneficial for children with ADHD. The same studies have shown that zinc and magnesium can be deficient in their systems as well. A good source of Zinc comes from red meat, seafood, peanuts and almonds. Foods rich in magnesium include nuts, cereal grains, peas, and green leafy vegetables.

Proteins and ADHD

A good way to reduce ADHD symptoms is to make sure that your child is receiving an adequate supply of protein several times a day, everyday. This will provide a steady supply of building blocks for neurotransmitters. It will unclog all of the unhealthy fats and help to balance the nervous and digestive systems.

Protein rich foods from the plant kingdom include soy, tofu, sunflower seeds, flax and flax seeds, almonds, walnuts, whole grains, beans, peas, lentils, mushrooms, seaweed and algae. Protein foods from the animal kingdom include egg whites, white and red meat and fish

Meal Planning

As elementary school age children go through physical changes their food intake becomes a critical aspect of their growth and development. Research shows that a nutritious diet not only makes a child healthier, it makes them emotionally more stable. This translates into improved school performance. It is up to us as parents to plan for a nutritious diet and to stick to it.

Breakfast

A child getting ready for a day in school requires a good breakfast. He/she has not eaten for about twelve hours and whether they know it or not their body is hungry. A doughnut or something of that fashion is not good enough as it only provides energy that lasts about 30-60 minutes. Some options include:

- Prepare a shake or smoothie with milk. There is quite a selection of blended breakfast drinks. You can then add bananas, wheat germ, algae etc. Research indicates that eight ounces of such a drink served with 2 slices of whole-wheat toast will prepare your child until his school lunch.

- If your child likes cereal, dry or cooked, give it an added boost with some wheat germ, nuts, raisins or some other fruit.

- Yogurt is great with some fruit or granola, or other dried cereal.

Lunch

That dreaded sack lunch. The big questions are, "are they eating their food and if so how much of it"? One clue is to watch and see if the fridge is attacked the moment they walk in the house after school. Sometimes lunches can get a little monotonous. Let's see if we can get a little more creative by asking your child what they would enjoy for lunch; allow them to help in planning the menus. If they will go, take them shopping with you. Remember to make the choices nutritious.

After School Snacks

This is a great opportunity to add some really healthy stuff to their diet. Try to avoid the sweet stuff. We know this is no good for the metabolism, and needless to say, our teeth suffer for it as well.

- Post a "what's inside for a snack" list and let the child help himself/herself.

- Keep a supply of nuts, raisins, and dried fruits. If you do not frequent health food stores, grocery stores now have huge selections of fresh snack foods to choose from. Dates, coconuts, prunes, apricots, sunflower seeds and almonds are all delicious and are but just a few.

- Fruit.

- Cheese with whole-wheat crackers is a favorite, but try to limit the intake of dairy products, as they are not good for allergies.

Dinner

- Here again allow the child to participate in the planning of their meals. Read some cookbooks together to come up with some delectable foods.

- Presentation is everything. Make the foods look attractive and if you are putting love into the preparation then it will be returned to you ten fold.

- Have the kid's help you prepare, make it a fun experience. Over time you will see how much this nurtures family relationships.

- Make this a sharing time. Turn off the TV's, stereos, computers, telephones or anything else that can interrupt. Make the dinner table a place for good conversation and communication.

Proper Nourishment During Pregnancy and "Why Breast Feed Your Baby"?

If you are pregnant or thinking of becoming pregnant you need to make sure you are getting good nutrition. The importance of nutrition for the health of the baby was clearly shown in an analysis of Dutch medical records from the Second World War. The German army embargoed all food supplies entering Holland; this caused a food shortage until the Allies liberated the area in 1945. One key finding was that in those babies that were conceived during this period there was an increase in the number of central nervous system dysfunctions, children exhibiting ADHD symptoms rose at an alarming rate. This indicates that nutritional deprivation, even long before pregnancy has a significant impact on both mother and child.

Pregnant mothers should incorporate adequate amounts of vitamin B and EFA's around time of conception and the first six weeks of pregnancy according to the Center for Disease Control, to ensure the health of their newborn.

Pregnancy plays a critical role in the immune system breakdown. Mothers who have a history of anemia, miscarriages, viruses, low protein diets, drug and alcohol abuse, cigarette smoking, low or high weight gain or who become pregnant under the age of 16 or over the age of 36 are considered at high risk. If any of these risk factors were present it would be wise for the mother to minimize stress and on the advice of your doctor, take 1000-5000 mg of vitamin C, 1000mg Calcium and 500-700 mg. of Magnesium and B complex daily.

After the birth it is highly recommended that you breast-feed your child for the first 9-24 months. Mother's milk which is the ultimate nourishment for newborns, contain these specific EFA's critical for brain and visual development.

A study done at Purdue University showed that there were significant differences between children who were breast-fed (mother's milk contains naturally contains the necessary EFA's) and those formula fed (no EFA's). Upon completion of this study EFA's were then incorporated into baby's formula making.

A General Review of What to Feed Yourself and Your Child

Taking into account the importance of addressing all six-organ systems that are likely to be involved in ADHD, we can suggest a list of recommended foods to adopt into your diet.

Anything rich in essential fatty acids, minerals, vitamins, chlorophyll, natural enzymes and protein would be good choices.

From the animal kingdom the most nutritious food is salmon. It has large amounts of protein, minerals, EFA's and algae oil. Other deepwater fish such as cod, mackerel and sardines are nutritious as well.

From the plant kingdom blue-green algae has over 100 nutrients, including essential fatty acids, minerals, bio-flavenoids, enzymes, chlorophyll, beta-carotene and B vitamins.

Use dark grains and whole grain flower, or sweeteners, again the darker the better with honey and molasses being the preferable choices.

Remember that although it is difficult to change any habit and you may initially feel resistant, this is by no means an insurmountable task. The key is the realization of what your body needs in order to function at top performance.

CHAPTER 10

The Effects of Exercise & Relaxation on Your Exceptional Child

THERE IS NO MAGIC

Do we need to be "drugging" our children or can we be managing certain learning, social and behavioral issues through an alternative means? The information that follows will offer insights, facts and research into exercise and relaxation techniques that you may wish to incorporate into the overall care of your child.

A growing number of specialists are suggesting that a regular program of physical exercise may lead to fewer children with symptoms of ADHD, and that it may lower or eliminate the need for the use of drugs to control this disorder.

The average child now sits in front of a television or computer screen for four to six hours per day. But most children learn best through techniques that use hands-on or experiential learning, which has been our primary mode of teaching up until recent history. When did this change and why?

In classroom studies, several researchers have found that the inclusion of exercise into the daily routine of a child has led to an increase of attention span, impulse control and that the frequency of classroom disruptions decreased by 50%. In addition, the studies found that children who were taking stimulant medication required less when they were exercising on a regular basis.

I was recently talking to a parent whose child had been diagnosed with ADHD. His nine-year-old son loved exercise and was an avid hockey player. I asked the parent if he observed any difference in his child's hyperactivity after a hockey practice. He thought for a second, his eyes brightened and he acknowledged a much better attention span, mood and ability to concentrate in his son after he had exercised.

A common problem for ADHD children is concentration during homework time and this child was no exception. During the day this nine-year-old's behavior was controlled with the use of Ritalin. It was quite a revelation to both the parent and child to see a significant difference in focusing with just the exercise. There was no need for medication to be taken at home.

Dr. Michael Wendt conducted a study on the effects of running and exercise on the behavior of ADHD children. The children ranged from five to twelve years of age and all were professionally diagnosed with ADHD. Wendt, who worked as a public school administrator, saw a correlation between exercise and behavior when it came to ADHD children. He observed that during the beginning of an athletic season, when practice sessions were intense, the behavior problems of these ADHD students did not occur as frequently as they did when practices focused less on conditioning.

Wendt's research showed a positive impact from intense exercise over a period of six weeks and most of the behavioral changes were noticed within the first two weeks.

The exercise program Wendt put together, was designed to have the following:

- A 10 minute warm-up

- A 10 minute cool down

- 20 minutes of exercise into a heart-rate zone of 135-175 beats per minute.

- The frequency of exercise was designed to be five out of seven days per week.

The research he conducted went on to indicate that children in North America were not getting enough exercise in recess, play or regular class time.

Wendt designed one of the activities that the children participated in during the week to include a long distance run. Many children ran between two and five miles during this session.

When a colleague shared his experience of having Kindergarten teachers refuse to let their children take part in a walking exercise because it was too far for them, Wendt was astonished. Those kindergarten children had only been asked to walk one lap around the track.

Wendt's research study was designed to go beyond what we presently expose our children to in normal settings. His study showed conclusive beneficial results of regular vigorous exercise.

Further Supporting Research

Extensive research has shown that blood flow is very important for brain development and that we can get the same results with intense exercise like running as we do from medication.

It has also been proven that by exercising on a regular basis you increase the production of neurotransmitters.

Neurotransmitters are important for good communication between the nerve cells. It can be compared to an artery that is clogged; thus reducing the blood flow and creating damage to our circulatory system. Without this efficient communication between the nerve cells, behavior and learning can break down. There is mounting research that outlines how exercise promotes the release of Dopamine, epinephrine and other body chemicals that have a positive impact on focusing and attention spans.

Exercising the Mind Body and Spirit

"By letting go of our fears and negativity and learning to see the best in ourselves and others we provide a powerful impetus for positive change. It is through our ability to go beyond pre-conceived notions and external appearances that we can transform our lives and those of our children[3]."

Sonia Sumar

We as parents and educators need to once again look at the merits of educating the mind, body and spirit of our present day children in unison.

Yoga for the Special Child

Yoga is a practice of physical and mental exercise that originated in India more than three thousand years ago. Its' purpose is to help us experience enduring physical and mental health. One practice of Yoga, taught in western culture is Hatha Yoga. Hatha Yoga begins by working with the body on a structural level, helping to align the vertebrae, increase flexibility and strengthen muscles. At the same time as the internal organs are being rejuvenated, the epidermal, digestive, lymphatic, cardiovascular and pulmonary systems are purified of toxins. The nervous and endocrine systems are balanced and the brain cells are nourished. The end result is increased mental clarity, emotional stability and a greater sense of overall well being.

Because Yoga works on these many different levels, it has potential as an effective therapy for conditions that do not respond well to conventional treatment. For this reason, children with ADHD, Down Syndrome and other developmental disabilities, who practice Yoga, often surprise their parents and instructors with their quick mastery of basic motor, communicative and thinking skills. The same Yoga can help children with learning disabilities develop greater levels of concentration, balance and composure in their daily lives.

Sonia Sumar has done a tremendous amount of work teaching Yoga to children who have special needs. Her Teaching Center and Yoga Studio are situated in Brazil.

Sonia tours and speaks of her work with Yoga directed to children with various disabilities. She bases her program on her experiences with her own daughter, Roberta, who was born with Down syndrome.

Sonia began Yoga practices with Roberta when she was just three months old. During first grade Roberta was given a battery of IQ and performance tests with the following results:

- Psychiatric, psychological, social behavior and learning ability tests, showed good results with near normal development for her age.

- Her IQ was scored at 87, which is considered borderline normal. She was functioning about 2 years behind others of her age group. Down Syndrome IQ's normally range from 20-55.

- Socially she was observed to have some difficulty communicating with classmates, but had good relationships with adults. She exhibited no behavioral problems.

- She had good relationships with her mother and sister. Father was absent.

- Although slow in her development, Roberta is receptive and educable. She was able to learn to read and write. She paid attention, displayed interest, and demonstrated good reasoning ability and comprehension.

It goes without saying that our children are our teachers, and Sonia quickly realized that Roberta was teaching her the development of her Yoga practice. Sonia recognized that her job was to be open and receptive to what Roberta's body was telling her it needed and credits Roberta for the development of the work she does with children with special needs.

In her work with these special children she divides the Yoga practices into four areas:

1. Asanas or body postures.

2. Pranayama.

3. Breathing exercises.

4. Music and sound therapy.

5. Deep relaxation

Asanas means "posture" or "pose." There are more than one hundred different Yoga poses which are divided into two categories, active and passive. The ACTIVE poses tone specific muscle groups, benefit organs, endocrine glands and activates brain cells. The PASSIVE poses are used in meditation, relaxation and pranayama practices. The greatest benefit from practicing these postural positions comes when we learn how to relax in a given position. It is said that real relaxation comes from deep concentration where the mind is focused on a single object. In this case the object is the body.

Pranayama is the science of breathing. Breath is the main source of nourishment for the cells in the body. We can live without food for weeks, without water for days, but without oxygen we cease to exist in a few short minutes. The average person uses about one seventh of their lung capacity. By learning how to increase this capacity we can increase the amounts of vital energy to all of our organs, build immunity to diseases and literally be in a position to control our own healing. Research indicates that when practiced consistently, pranayama can help to balance our emotions and mind. Try an experiment by sitting quietly with no distractions. What you will probably experience is a myriad of sensations and thoughts, which are uncontrollable. The practice of pranayama allows for us to quiet our minds and bodies and truly be able to relax, surrender unwanted feelings, clear mental blockages and create overall healing for ourselves.

Music and sound therapy uses rhythm, combined with hand movements to develop concentration, breath coordination, communication and motor skills and the music itself has a calming effect on the nervous system.

Deep Relaxation is the conclusion of the session. For 10-20 minutes the body just relaxes with no movement. This allows for the body to fully experience what it has just gone through.

Relaxation techniques can vary:

- By focusing on individual parts of our bodies we can use our minds to help in the release of physical tensions and mental stress.

- We learn to use visualization and meditation techniques to allow the release of these areas of tension and blockages.

- There are several breathing techniques designed to help our bodies relax and promote clarity of our minds. Very often breathing is used as a prelude to meditation.

Relaxation is a very powerful meditation practice, which leads to a greater sense of peace, harmony and well being within our lives.

Children with ADHD experience social and learning delays due to their hyperactivity and distractibility. Depending on their ages and stage of development, Yoga teachers will introduce pranayama and some asanas as part of their initial Yoga routine. This helps to calm them so that they are better able to follow instructions.

Breathing Exercises, which include:

The Cleansing Breath - The cleansing breath removes excess mucus from the sinuses and respiratory tract. It clears stale air from the lungs and replaces it with highly oxygenated air. The result is that it raises oxygen levels in the blood, which increases our ability to focus. The cleansing breath is especially good for children with asthma and sinus conditions.

The technique for the cleansing breath is:

- One normal inhalation, followed by

- A rapid exhalation. The air is expelled from the lungs by a forceful, inward and upward movement.

- Always breathe through the nostrils with the mouth closed. Breathing through the nostril helps to filter the warm air, before it enters the lungs.

- Continue this for 20 inhalations and 20 exhalations.

- Take a break and then repeat the process one or two more times.

- Place your child's hand and yours over their belly. Show them how the stomach moves in and out during the exercise.

- Ask them how they feel after the practice and watch for any signs of dizziness.

The Bellows Breath - is a highly energizing, rapid breathing exercise. It fills the lungs with freshly oxygenated air as well as creating a better environment for all of our organs. It strengthens the diaphragm, warms the body, increases circulation and aids in digestion.

The technique is:

- A rapid inhalation followed by a rapid exhalation.

- Repeat without pausing between the inhalation and exhalation.

- Breathe through the nostrils.

- By placing your child's hand and yours over theirs, show them how the stomach moves in and out during the exercise.

- Explain to them all of the great things that this is doing for their body.

- Do 20-25 inhalations and exhalations.

- At the end of the set have the child take a slow deep breath.

- Repeat this two more times.

Alternate Nostril Breathing - is known as the "Nerve Purification Breath." This is a great exercise for the "quieting" of the mind. The breath strengthens the entire nervous system and helps to balance the right and left hemispheres of the brain leaving us with a greater sense of awareness and security and better prepared for our day. Additionally it strengthens our immune system, stimulates digestion and develops better concentration.

The technique is:

- Demonstrate to your child by taking your right hand and holding your thumb and first finger together so that it makes the shape of an, "O".

- Press the end of these two fingers in on your right nostril, closing off that pathway.

- Inhale deeply through your left nostril to the count of 10.

- Then release your right nostril and simultaneously with your other three fingers seal off your left nostril and exhale to the count of 10 through your right nostril.

- Now reverse and breathe deeply and inhale with your right nostril having pressed the end of the thumb and first finger together and on the left nostril.

- Release your left nostril; sealing your right nostril with the other 3 fingers.

- Repeat this process for 5-6 rounds.

If you can build up to 10-20 minutes of breathing techniques per day, you will truly have a much healthier mind and body. You will have achieved a very important practice on the way to a greater sense of peace and harmony in your life.

Relaxation and Visualization Techniques for Calming the Mind, Body and Soul

The information here is for anyone who is living lives of stress and challenges on a daily basis. Are you aware that we are probably the only animal on our planet that continues to survive while living with such high amounts of stress and challenges on a daily basis? We are surviving, but stress definitely takes its toll on us physically and mentally and it's sad that we typically only consider doing something about controlling it when our bodies begin to break down.

Should we be proud that we have found ways to adapt to these extreme levels of duress? Should we feel accomplished that we have found ways to medicinally treat the symptoms of stress? Perhaps another way to look at it would be to relieve the stress that causes the symptoms before it gets as far as requiring medical treatment.

The human body is designed to live for a considerably longer period of time than we are currently surviving. We can attain these life spans through proper diet, exercise and by being in control of the stress, rather than having it control us.

The following are alternatives and preventatives that both you and your child can participate in to aid you in creating a calmer and more peaceful way of life. If practiced on a regular basis, they WILL relax your mind and body and release your inner tensions. Ultimately these strategies will empower both you and your child with a greater sense of calm, clarity, organization, peace and self-control.

Laughter

Laughter is one of the best methods used to release stress. During laughter neuro-chemicals called Serotonin and Beta-endorphin are produced and released into the blood stream. Although it is not yet known precisely how, through scientific studies we do know that the right balance of neuro-chemicals is what maintains our mood and sanity. Not only do these natural stimulants have the ability to work on our brain to give us that natural high feeling but they are also the main chemicals that the body releases to reduce pain and tension. Laughter has been shown to alleviate many conditions including anxiety, depression, addiction, allergies and even contribute to the positive prognosis in cancer sufferers. There is no substitute for the natural healing qualities of laughter and it definitely is the one condition we would like to infect others with, especially our children.

Meditation

Meditation is one of the most beneficial self-help techniques that you can implement for yourself and your child. Throughout a typical day, dealing with issues from home, work, children, families and friends can over tax and unbalance us. Finding ways of unloading the stress we put on ourselves should be one of the main focuses we have.

The exercise of meditation may take some practice but everyone, no matter what the age most definitely can utilize it.

Clearing ones mind of all unpleasantness and concentrating on simple, peaceful thoughts, not allowing worries and concerns to enter the picture and finding that inner place of peace is the main objective of meditating.

In the beginning the art of focusing may take some patience and practice. When other thoughts interrupt, allow them to leave as quickly as they appeared. Put them into a balloon and watch them float away. One of the keys is to concentrate on getting your body to relax. Visualize your muscles relaxing, the tension being released from your neck, your shoulders, your solar plexus, hips and knees. Wherever you may be feeling it. You will get to know your body very well and automatically send relaxing energy to the places that require it. Some people find that chanting a word or phrase or counting your breaths help with the focusing.

Just like many practices there are different levels of meditation that your mind will go through. Each level happens automatically as you go deeper and become more relaxed. There is no wrong way to meditate, just as there is no one correct way. Find the method that is comfortable for you.

These are only some very basic guidelines to help you get started:

- Find a comfortable place to meditate. Create a warm, caressing and peaceful environment for yourself. You'll want to remain comfortable for the duration, so seat yourself knowing that every part of your body is supported properly yet not so comfortably that you immediately fall to sleep. You may wish to have candles lit, soft music playing and fragrance to help stimulate your senses. Others should be told that it is not acceptable to interrupt you and all phones should be turned off. As you become more practiced in meditation you will find that absolutely nothing will interrupt your process, you will just automatically tune everything else out.

- The ideal time to meditate each day is before your daily routine has a chance to put a lot of stress on you. You'll find that after a consistent meditation practice, very little will be able to throw you out of balance and if something does, it will only take a few moments to refocus your energy and any tensions will easily slip away.

- Sitting with the spine straight up is the recommended posture. The neck should be elongated with your chin at about a 90-degree angle to your body. If you find that you are getting sleepy, change your posture slightly.

- In the beginning meditate for short periods, maybe 10-15 minutes and gradually work up to an amount of time that feels comfortable to you.

- As you practice you will refine the technique that best fits your style and body. Allow for this to be your sacred space and time for rejuvenation.

Breath Work

Breathing techniques are an invaluable tool for relaxation whether used in conjunction with Yoga, meditation and other exercise or on its own. Learning to breathe your way through stressful situations allows for time to STOP and to look at things from a different perspective. Once you train yourself and your child to do this you'll find that you will see a reduction in impulsive behaviors and rash decisions. Just a few minutes of deep breathing techniques will send more oxygen to the cells throughout your body, slowing your heart rate and creating more clarity and an overall sense of calmness.

A simple breathing technique that can be used by anyone, at any time, is to sit or stand in a relaxed position and slowly inhale through your nose for a count of four and hold for another count of four. Now slowly exhale through your mouth to the same count. Repeat this several times while you feel the pressure easing. Allow the breath to move right from your base of your spine, up through your body and through the top of your head. Visualize it traveling through every cell, energizing them as it does. Let the breath escape through the crown of your head bringing with it all of the tensions you were feeling. Relax and bring your breath back to a regular pace. The great thing about breathing is that it can be used absolutely anywhere, at any time.

Please refer to the section on Yoga for more in depth breathing techniques.

Sound Therapy

Certain sounds have pronounced effects on our brain wave patterns. Sound therapy revitalizes and has a harmonizing and healing effect on almost every aspect of our body. We can access and utilize natural sounds all around us as nature has a vast repertoire of soothing and rhythmic sounds. Take for example the sounds of the ocean, rustling of leaves, a waterfall, the wind blowing or just the sound of silence. Listen and journey deeper into tranquility as it moves through your body.

The East Indian practice of chanting is considered to be relaxing and meditative and in Native American culture the combination of chanting, dancing and drumming has been used for centuries as their method of tapping into their inner sub-consciousness for relaxation, greater clarity and for opening the mind and body to spiritual experiences.

Sound therapy has been found to help individuals with:

- Eliminating fatigue.
- Increasing energy and vitality.

- Deep relaxation, causing the healing of stress related disorders such as high blood pressure and digestive problems.

- Increased focus and concentration.

- Easier and more effective sleep.

Visualization Techniques

Visualization techniques have been widely used for goal setting and self-healing. Visualizing images which are beautiful and peaceful; a beach, a starry moonlit night in a huge empty field, a garden full of flowers on a clear, warm sunlit afternoon are just a few examples.

Visualize yourself on a deserted beach, a sunny and warm day, with a gentle breeze blowing. The waves are gently breaking in on the beach. As the wind blows over your body, it is blowing your tensions out towards the water as the waves take them away. With each gust of wind goes another level of tension and you feel a little more relaxed

Visualizations have been practiced to reduce and control pain, lower blood pressure, cure phobias and set goals of any kind whether it is for a career, financial security or romance. The first step is to see yourself there and actually believe it's possible. Visualizing yourself making a perfect golf swing, following the football into your hands or winning that race affirms that you believe you are capable of the task and actually increases your ability to carry through and create that reality.

It has helped people wishing to stop smoking. They associate a lung that is black and filled with unhealthy smoke each time they inhale on a cigarette and before long they feel ill every time they take a puff.

Walking to Release Stress

We know that tension, anxiety and anger can be overwhelming feelings and very self-destructive to our health and relationships. These negative emotions can be reduced by taking long walks.

Walking provides you with an excellent opportunity to invigorate your body and release muscular tensions through the additional intake of oxygen. Long walks exercise your heart, lungs, digestive system and muscular system and provides you with time and space to think clearly.

A good walking regiment will include the following:

- Begin at a moderate pace and then increase your speed to a comfortable level as you go. Set your eyes to the middle ground 6-8 feet ahead of you. A slower pace at first also allows for your feelings and thoughts to open up.

- As you pick up the pace you feel more energetic and your thinking process improves as well. You begin to find solutions to problems, as you see things with greater clarity or perhaps you'll choose to forget whatever you were stressed about in the first place.

- At the end, as you slow and cool down you will notice how your mind and body have become relaxed and peaceful.

Regular walking sessions can increase self-esteem, improve your physical and mental discipline and keep your body healthy and in the process you are releasing blocked energy and negative feelings and thoughts.

Effects of Sports on the ADHD Child

ADHD children can benefit from sporting activities in many ways. One thing we know is that vigorous activity releases endorphins, the brain chemical that reduces stress and enhances over all well-being. This is particularly important for children with ADHD. Sports can also teach social skills, organizational skills and develop self-esteem. It goes without saying that it helps to keep the body fit. Sports such as, swimming, tennis, gymnastics, Yoga, wrestling, Tai Chi, and karate are some examples of the programs that are available within your community.

For many children, the most formidable opponents are themselves as they exhibit the same difficulties on the field as they do in the classroom. Team sports may not work as well as they seem to challenge a child's already low frustration tolerances, especially when the child does not come out a winner.

These children do well in sports where they can get a considerable amount of individual attention. It becomes easier for them to focus when they have that one-on-one relationship with their instructor. Activities that promote discipline and control like Tai Chi, Karate or Chi Gung are especially beneficial to the learning disabled child. These sports are about self-discipline and control. The movements teach them about their bodies and there is also an element of meditation and relaxation. The combination of mind, body and spirit are worked into unison and harmony.

The Chinese martial art of Tai Chi has been used as a non-pharmacological alternative therapy for ADHD children. Adult studies reveal that Tai Chi reduces symptoms associated with stress anger and confusion. In addition it improves balance and provides a sense of well being.

Music and Dance to Soothe the Restless Soul

The effect that the combination of music and dance has on the body, mind and spirit is invaluable. As a participant in dance, I have seen the total transformation that adults and children have gone through as a result of letting themselves be moved and swept away in dance. It is as if this combination has a direct link to one's soul. It provides a medium for the opportunity for inner transformation that traditional therapy can't reach. People get in touch with their emotions and bodies as they flow to the natural rhythm of the music. It is the one individual activity that has the ability to train the brain in an area that academics just cannot reach. One's heart becomes lighter, it reduces stress, provides structure and it is an activity that puts a smile on your face as well as in your heart.

I have recently read an article about an ADHD child who registered to do ballet and tap dance. Although she just wanted to attend for the fun of it, she quickly found herself addicted to this new activity. For the first time in her life she developed real friendships, her grades began improving and after her first recital, she felt a huge sense of accomplishment. Her life began to take on a positive outlook, which had never existed previously. In addition she developed a sense of commitment and responsibility to her dance and she began to mirror this in other areas of her school and home life.

Dancing opens up new areas emotionally and provides structure, demands focus and concentration and it forces coordination of the attention centers in the brain. Learning new dances, experiencing movements that you didn't think your body could do, finding new sources of energy, when combined, all act together to build self confidence and a feeling of mastery and self accomplishment.

Dance may not be for everyone but with some experimentation we all can find some area of exercise that is enjoyable. Something that provides a little more lightness into our lives, something that is fun and heartwarming. Is that not what life is all about? Just one more wonderful opportunity for us to experience the sense that the MAGIC is in the fact that that there really is NO MAGIC to it at all.

CHAPTER 11

Management & Motivation

In every child who is born,
under no matter what circumstances,
and of no matter what parents,
the potentiality of the
human race is born again.

James Agee

Our Role in Managing and Motivating Our Child

Even though we will talk predominantly about the child who has various learning challenges the information here can and does apply to anyone who is raising a family.

Normal parenting styles would have us either bringing up our children in the same manner as we were raised or more probably by the "trial and error" method. There are many books, this one included, on the subject of parenting and enough counselors and coaches who would make it seem like they have all of the answers. It is very simple really. That is, once you realize that there is no one book, nor is there any one all-knowing person better than yourself to decide how best to raise your child.

Books and counselors can only be used as guidelines. They are tools to be used to provoke thoughts or bring you new ideas that you may not have thought of, or perhaps be the support you may look for when you are faced with difficult times. You are in charge of parenting your child for better or worse.

Where Do We Start

I remember when my wife and I brought home our first child, an absolutely adorable daughter we named Jenna. Three days later we were walking through the front door of our home with her in one of those carryalls that convert into a hundred different things. We were filled with love and pride for her and so much apprehension about being the perfect parents. We put her down on the kitchen table and stared in amazement. We looked at her and then at each other, and both said simultaneously..."well, now what do we do", and burst into laughter. I can honestly say that at that time I knew more about taking that carryall and making it into all of the things it could become, than I did about raising this beautiful little girl. What were we to do?

As a parent, we can honestly, and in some cases painfully, say that each and every moment of child rearing comes with that exact question...WHAT DO WE DO NEXT?

People plan for their careers, their financial future, vacations and details about life both at home and on the job, but how much real consideration is given to parenthood? Sure, there is thought given to the preparation of the baby's room, what the child's name will be and who will be the one to take time off to care for the child and that sort of thing. How many parents sit down and work out a parenting plan? Do many speak to their significant other in order to determine their points of view on parenting?

I'm no exception. I went into parenthood blindly, just hoping for the best. In hindsight, I now see how things could have come about much simpler and with a lot less misunderstandings had my wife and I set out with a plan, or at the very least, knew what each other's philosophies were. How can we leave something so important to chance? Yet when it comes to parenting we seem to have this void, we take so much for granted and generally feel that everything will just fall into place.

You won't be capable of planning for everything that will come up in your parenting careers, but having an idea of where each other stands on certain issues and having a general game plan set up for the overall upbringing of your child will make parenting a lot less stressful. Know your plans for schooling, for childcare, nutrition and healthcare, the budget restrictions that will have to be considered.

The world today is fast paced and full of expectation. Our days are filled with organizing, managing and making sure that things flow smoothly for everyone. Sometimes motivating ourselves to even get up in the morning to face the day can be a challenge. Go easy on yourselves. Being a burned out super-mom/dad is not what your children really want. They're looking for someone who is human; someone who is "okay" with making a mistake. This sets a safe space for them to experiment and be all right when things don't quite go as they had planned. There is no failure, except for not trying in the first place.

We are looking to teach our children discipline, self-esteem (for themselves as well as others), courage, compassion, understanding and a sense of responsibility. We are looking to build a core for this child that will allow them to proceed into this world as a strong, knowing and confident individual. This is not something that can be taught from any manual, course or lecture. It is something we show our child through example. You are their teacher, mentor and advocate.

We teach this through offering a caring, firm, supportive and consistent environment. We make ourselves accessible and are there emotionally and spiritually for them to provide for a healthier, happier and solid family unit.

Keys to Positive Discipline

Do you know the difference between punishment and discipline?

Punishment: To inflict pain or loss. To cause pain, loss or some discomfort to a person because of some fault or offence.

Discipline: The training, especially of the mind or character. The ultimate training effect of experience.

We often confuse the word discipline with punishment. It is through disciplining our children, that we will teach them values and setting their boundaries. This can, and should, always be done in a constructive, nurturing and caring, but firm manner. Through this, self-control, self-esteem and responsibility are manifested and ingrained in your child.

Effective strategies that can provide discipline while nurturing the dignity and grace within your child are through:

Setting limits - Parents must set limits for their children. No one else can discipline with the same love and affection and caring as a parent. Knowing where their boundaries are allows the child a sense of safety and security. They are naturally more comfortable with regular routines where they know what is expected of them. Sit with your child and decide certain consequences for negative behaviors. Allow them to be aware of the consequence that will occur if they go beyond the set limit prior to them finding themselves in the situation.

Discipline - It is the parent's gift to their child to see that they experience the consequence of his or her own behavior. Consequence is one of the best teaching methods available. Allow your child to see that they are in control of their own outcomes. Giving your child choices while letting them know what the outcome will be will provide them with experience in good decision-making vs. poor decision-making.

Remember to acknowledge when your child makes a good choice, and praise them for it. Positive reinforcement is so important to the esteem of everyone and I cannot stress enough how important I find it to be in the parenting of a child. Find something to praise in your child at least three times during the day. As a matter of fact find something to praise yourself for. Yes, pat yourself on the back. You are doing a wonderful job at parenting this amazing child you have. Feeling good about yourself? This is exactly how your child will feel from the praise they receive from you. It may be all the encouragement they need.

Avoid power struggles with a child, for this just shows your child that you are not in control of the situation. Power struggles are just another way for us to exert control, and control is exactly what we are trying not to teach here. We want them to learn from the outcomes and consequences of their decisions. We want to reinforce the situation where our children can learn more about themselves from their own experiences and through good decision-making.

Empty threats - We've all done this. If we allowed ourselves to look, we'd see how foolish we are for doing it. We could actually have a good laugh at our own expense when we look back at some of the outrageous, emotionally charged and frustrating, empty threats we've made.

Making threats, which cannot be carried out, is worse than futile. At best, threats just show our kids that we are feeling helpless and hopeless. Kids will become defiant to worthless threats because they already know the truth, which is that we have no intention of carrying them out in the first place. We've lost composure and control of the situation. The child can then challenge the threat and show us who is really in control. Is this what we want? A wise parent will not make any statements that cannot be followed through. I wish you good luck with this one because once again, for some of us it may be easier said than practiced.

Children may not believe what we say,
but will always believe everything we do!

Elaine Gibson

The key to it is to take the emotion out of discipline by not lecturing, arguing, or raising your voice. Your job is to set the limits, the consequences and then **FOLLOW THROUGH!** Punishment will not work but **DISCIPLINE** will!

Parental Authority

If at all, we wish to convey a sense of authority in a positive way. To be authoritative, is to show through our attitude, body language, our tone of voice and the volume with which we speak, what it is that we wish from our child. My suggestion is that it be done in a consistent, firm, and loving manner. These are the qualities that we wish to use when conveying authority to our child.

If there is a hint of fear, tentativeness, confusion, begging, pleading or anger in our voice, then our authority is lost as the child can clearly see that we have lost our composure. I have seen countless numbers of times where children as young as a year old are literally running their families, because the parent was afraid to assert their authority. In this case the child will seize control because they know that the adult is obviously not the one in charge.

We can be kind to children and still be firm, but our expectations must be clear right from the beginning. When a child has no choice, then no options should be given to them.

An example of this is when it is time for supper and Jackie is called to come to sit down at the table and Jackie says, "I'll be there in 1 second" and keeps on playing. Five minutes later, Jackie is called once again, and again Jackie says, "I'll be right there". The parent then tries to convince Jackie to come to the table and a confrontation occurs.

When it is time to eat, the parent must let the child know what the expectations and consequences are.

What we are not realizing in this situation is that by allowing this situation to occur we are sending out the message that this is acceptable behavior. We are teaching our children how to be defiant. The term that is used to describe the behavior is "oppositional defiance".

We know that parenting is never simple, but perhaps these suggestions will assist you in making your wishes known to your child:

- Make your expectations clear;

- Talk and act like a parent who is in control and has self-control;

- Believe in and institute a gentle but firm way of delivering your authority;

- Help the child follow through with your expectation of them; and

- Be prepared to carry out the consequence if they don't.

This is a time when your child is learning from you. Remember to be consistent, be firm and be loving. Your patience in this will work miracles in the raising of your child.

> Don't be afraid to be boss
> Children are constantly
> testing, attempting to see
> how much they can get
> away with - how far you
> will let them go - And they secretly hope
> you will not let them go far.

Ann Landers

Setting Up Your Own Behavioral Plan

You will initially want to identify what the behavior problems are and then start working on them one behavior at a time.

Identify those behavior cycles that your child is displaying on a continuing basis. Prior to initiating a change you will need to understand that you play a part in precipitating this behavior. Know what your role in it is and be open to the possibility of making a change within yourself in order to alter your child's behavior. Sometimes simply in shifting your reaction, you create the desired shift within your child.

What is it exactly that you wish to change? Set boundaries that show clear limits and will encourage self-control within your child. Allow them to participate in the process of determining appropriate consequences. Giving your child an explanation of the consequences helps for them to make conscious choices and it hones in on developing their decision-making skills.

Empower your child by encouraging them to realize that they are in control of their own outcomes.

Any behavioral plan is based on two important concepts. First, you are more likely to succeed in changing behavior by rewarding what is desired than by punishing what is undesired. Secondly, for a plan to work, your responses to acceptable and unacceptable behaviors must be consistent. You must continue the program until you are absolutely certain that the unacceptable behavior is gone. Inconsistencies in your responses will actually increase the behavior that you wish to stop. As you know, there is no right or wrong here, what is important is to work together with other parenting authorities in the home to develop this plan.

None of the above can be accomplished through **reasoning, bargaining, bribing, threatening or trying to provoke guilt.** You must already know that if you "step into the arena", play your child's game and agree to debate or argue with your child, you lose.

If you say that it is time to go to sleep and your child says, "But just another 15 minutes, please, pretty please," the answer must be, "I said that now is the time for bed". If you argue or relent about the 15 minutes, then it will soon become much more than just an additional 15 minutes, and soon your frustration and anger will result in additional confrontations and defiance. Now is not the time to be building in flexibility.

Planning Your Intervention Strategies

Overwhelmed? Are you confused, exhausted and frustrated as to why nothing has worked and that things seem to be getting worse?

Knowing that action needs to be taken but not quite knowing what to do can create stress and tension between you and your spouse. You may not quite agree as to what strategies should be used or what will work given the situation. When this happens, stop for a moment, literally take a breath and a break.

The first step is to collect data on your observations of the behavior. Each of the parenting figures should collect data separately so you can compare. It is important to do this baseline so you may begin to change things from the way you see them as having happened.

To collate the data you may wish to develop a chart. This chart will be used to record the particular behavior, the antecedent (what happened just before the behavior occurred) and the resulting consequence for the inappropriate behavior.

Date and Time:
_____ , ___ at __:__ am/pm
Antecedent:
Behavior:
Consequence:

Everyone involved will have different lists which will reflect the different parenting styles you use. For example one may be a disciplinarian and the other maybe more laid-back. Whichever way you deal with it is neither right nor wrong. The important goal is that each of you agrees on what the expectations are for the child and that the both of you are being consistent in asking that they be met.

Inconsistency reinforces the poor behavior, Consistency stops it.

In keeping track of your child's cycles, you will begin to see a pattern of that specific behavior.

Physical - (hitting or throwing)

Verbal - (Yelling, teasing, cursing, threatening)

Noncompliance - (Not listening to what is said, not doing what is requested, being openly defiant)

Once the cycle is identified, it is useful to recognize the patterns. For example does the behavior occur when the child is hungry, not feeling well or tired? Is the behavior occurring when the child comes from school, when he/she has missed their medication or when they are around a certain person? Is it related to academic performance or possibly the type of parenting style?

Setting Up the Plan

At this stage, define the behavior as clearly as possible and work out a consequence that will be carried out in a consistent fashion. Once the plan is put on paper introduce it to the family. The plan should be consistent among all siblings. Even if the behavior pattern is not for all the children, it will benefit them to be aware of consequences and/or the reward for their behavior.

The plan you create should be divided into 3 steps:

1. Create a schedule and divide the day into intervals. Wake-up time until departure for school, arrival from school until after supper and after supper to bedtime. Weekends can be divided into 4 parts with the meals as the dividers.

2. List the behavior(s) that you are focusing on.

3. The purpose of the plan is to reinforce positive behaviors, which can be done in several ways. You can set up a point system, whereby if the behavior does not

occur during a specific interval, then the child will receive a point, or a sticker. It can be anything that will motivate the child to want to receive the reward. You can also use verbal praise and in most cases will use both together, which of course works best.

A scenario that implements this practice could be:

Elliott gets up in the morning, completes all of his responsibilities, but calls his sister, "stupid". So Elliot gets his points for completing his tasks and for not hitting. You may say "Elliott, I am pleased that you earned two points for following the rules, tidying up and for not hitting this morning. I wish I could have given you your third point, but you did call your sister a name".

You may also say to Cathy "Cathy, I am happy that you earned all 3 of your points. Thank you for not calling your brother a name, after he called you one."

Can you see here that behavior is being changed by rewarding appropriate behavior from the child and not by punishing their wrongdoing?

A system is set up where the points are counted daily and recorded on a chart. The points can be used either daily, weekly or even a special reward for a major accomplishment.

Having the child participate in developing the rewards will create the excitement to then accomplish the task, but, all final decisions on the type of reward and whether or not the child has earned the reward will be made by you. There will be those children who will say, "this is stupid and I am not doing it". You will need to respond to this firmly and let them know that the system is going ahead, and if they would like an input on the reward for proper behavior they will need to participate or have you make the final decision without their input.

Each reward is individualized to the specific child's likes and desires.

Time Out Procedures

Before starting this plan, define which behaviors will be considered so unacceptable to the family that the result will not only be not earning a point, but also being removed from the family for a limited time. The "Time Out" strategy, one that you have probably used many times over already, is one of the best. It provides time for everyone involved to cool down and rethink things. Be sure to designate a specific room that is not equipped with a television, stereo, games or other pleasurable distractions. The door should remain closed and the child quiet. Make the period of time for the time out fit the misbehavior. Longer times for more serious situations and shorter for minor infractions. Each time the door is opened, the child yells, screams, or has a tantrum the clock should start over.

For the plan to work communication must be clear, consistent and absolutely firm.

It is important to realize that while implementing any new behavioral management system that initially, there will probably be an increase in the unacceptable behavior. This may make things seem hopeless and futile. You will probably feel that you are in a war and the reality is that you are in a battle, not only with your child but likely with yourselves as well. This is one time that you must take a stand if you wish to create positive change.

You may want to reassure your child by saying, "I will always be here to support you and love you, but when you choose this behavior I will not choose to participate with you".

Although it may interfere with family plans and routines, it is very important to maintain no interaction or communication with the child in any way until after the time out. At that point it will be very beneficial for them to be able to express, quietly and calmly, what brought on the behavior; how they felt before during and after; and most importantly, how they intend to deal with the situation the next time it crops up.

While continuing to do external reinforcing through time outs and reward systems, at some point you will wish to combine it with a more interactive relationship between the child and yourself. Begin talking about the behaviors and the progress in their ability to make the necessary behavior modifications. A good time to do this is at the end of the day, just before bedtime. You can use this period to reflect on the day and teach better self-management and decision-making skills. Your child will learn from hearing you openly discuss how you feel about things and what your thoughts are on how things are going. Make a point of broaching the topic from a removed point of view, rather than from the drama of the day.

You are now becoming the role model, teaching alternative ways for your son/daughter on how to deal with their actions and feelings. We are sometimes quick to tell our children not to show anger or disappointment. Anger is a normal feeling, yes you may want to yell, but don't abuse anyone; you might stamp your feet, but do not break anything. We exhibit these behaviors during frustrating times and children need to know they can do it as well, provided it is done in an appropriate way.

Teaching Self-Management to the ADHD Child

A Case Study 1

This is an actual observation of an ADHD child in his classroom.

The teacher directed her class to put away their drawings and line up at the door. While the other students were following her directions, Mark continued to work. He stood near his desk, moving around it in quick steps to add different touches to his artwork. The teacher noticed Mark's tardiness and immediately raised her voice and said "Mark, I said put it away, now!"

Mark looked up, startled, and he seemed unable to decide how to organize his stuff. After a few seconds he simply tossed handfuls of supplies into his desk. By this time, the other students had lined up by the door. Mark left his desk and walked in the general direction of his classmates. On the way he noticed that everyone in the class was already in line for recess. The teacher was already at the door with her arms folded, glaring straight at him. He ran toward the line but the teacher caught him and made him stay behind. She told him that she was tired of his not following directions and that he needed to stay in at recess to "think about it".

This scenario is typical of the daily chain of events that affects, tens of thousands of children diagnosed with ADHD and their teachers. In addition we have a tendency to deal with these behaviors in a reactionary manner, providing punishment rather than effective alternatives and instruction.

Teaching self-management allows for these children to take more and more responsibility for controlling their own behavior. The key elements in a successful self-management program are our ability to teach and model appropriate behavior while providing positive feedback to the child. Set up your expectations for them in a series of steps that they clearly understand and will be able to measure progress from.

To ensure Mark's success, the teacher in the above situation might have chosen to allow adequate cleanup time for Mark and given him a cue as to when it was appropriate for him to begin preparing for recess. Choosing to write down in detail on a flash card what her expectations of him would have allowed him to refer back to it to be sure he wasn't missing something important. By having an understanding of Mark's weak areas, and working with him to see that these issues were addressed, positive results would have been the outcome. Simply acknowledging that he attempted to do what was expected, by saying, " Mark, thank you for getting on line with, us. I see it took you a little longer today, try to improve next time" would have encouraged him to at least try harder.

By employing what is called "successive approximations", (as we move closer step by step to the desired behavior we apply the reinforcement) we allow for Mark to achieve success in a positive fashion. This ultimately is nurturing his self-esteem, fostering growth and developing his relationship with himself, his teacher and his classroom environment.

Giving Directions

Guidelines will help your child understand the process and follow through on instructions thereby empowering them and teaching them better self-management skills.

Try any or all of the following and see which work best for you and your child.

- It is important to get your child's complete attention.

- Touching or cueing them, bring them into direct focus with you.

- Do not compete with distractions such as television, stereo, computer, telephones or anything else that will distract the child from completely understanding your directions.

- Show your child what you want them to do, and role-play it if necessary so they know exactly what is expected of them.

- If required, break down tasks into smaller steps. Remember you want to guarantee success.

- Know your child and the number of directions they can take at one time.

- Try putting down on flash cards, what you want done, use pictures if necessary.

- Color code directions in order of priority.

- Keep all directions very brief and to the point.

- For young children, draw pictures that show the sequence of events.

- Always check whether the instructions have been understood. Many of these children have short-term memory difficulties.

- Provide follow-up and give frequent praise.

Don't show frustration when directions are not fully followed. Remember that many ADHD children have difficulty in disengaging from activities. They do not do well with transitioning and changes in their routine and they have poor memory recall.

Once you have provided the necessary structure, support and guidance, it is important that your child work independently to the best of their ability and that they are recognized for that. Remember practice is always the key to anything when we want to see improvement.

Working with the Hyperactive or Impulsive behaviors of your ADHD Child

These children cannot control their unpredictable and impulsive behavior. They become excited, over-aroused and because they cannot see the entire picture, do not understand why or how they have gotten themselves into these problem situations. Life is a disorganized, poorly timed blur to them. One cannot always place demands on these children to perform and behave without expecting some defiance and agitation.

- Impose the necessary expectations, limits, boundaries and reinforcements as we have discussed. This is absolutely crucial to the management and well-being, and success of your child.

- One of the lessons here for a parent to have is a greater understanding and awareness of their child's limitations.

- Know your child's behavioral patterns. Learn as much as you can about ADHD, it will help you to be more tolerant and compassionate. It helps to know that the behaviors they are exhibiting are not deliberate.

- Look for warning signs and learn to anticipate when your child is becoming over-stimulated or frustrated. Do this so that you may be able to intervene before any further agitation occurs.

- Teach your child strategies for self-management and control. Make sure these strategies are implemented whenever they are needed.

- Be conscious of when your child is exhibiting desired behaviors and reward them for it.

- Always take immediate action and be consistent in your discipline. Your child will then know what will occur for inappropriate behaviors.

- Provide a place where your child can calm down and get themselves back under control.

- Encourage socialization. Other children are good teachers and icebreakers.

- Anticipate the probability of accidents and damage. Arrange the environment to minimize such events.

- You need to model patience, understanding, flexibility, communication, and problem solving whenever possible.

- Model to your child the importance of expressing their feelings and provide times and safe space during the day for them to do so.

- Provide your child with plenty of exercise and opportunities to release their boundless amounts of energy. We know that a vigorous exercise program can have the same effect as a stimulant medication.

- Adjust your expectations for yourself and your child. Allow your child to develop at whatever academic and social level they are at rather than what the standard is or what you may feel is appropriate.

Being a parent and living with a hyperactive child is a huge challenge. We all know this. It is important for you to learn these strategies, follow through and be consistent, but above all else be gentle and patient with yourself. You will then have a much easier time in relating and in being understanding of your child's needs when you are well taken care of yourself.

Anticipating Behavior Problems in Public

Parents of children with ADHD can sometimes get to the point of dreading to go out in public for fear of embarrassing scenes. Subconsciously, the social pressures and expectations we put on our ADHD child can at times be the cause of what puts them over the edge. Here are some suggestions on how to help in these situations.

- Prior to going out in public, discuss and practice appropriate behavior. Anticipate potential problems and discuss them. Set limits and consequences for them. State the rules, and have your child repeat them back to you.

- Establish rewards for appropriate behavior.

- Do not put your child into situations that you know will be too taxing on their self-control and attention spans.

- If possible, prior to going out have your child exercise.

- Remove your child at the first signs of losing control. They may need some natural time out to wind down and then will find it easier to re-engage.

- When you see something happening, try to re-focus, bring a game or toy or book. Sometimes getting them involved in another activity helps.

- Give your child feedback and support.

Pitfalls

During the course of my twenty-something years of experience, I have observed some common pitfalls and will share them with you here.

If the child is not capable of achieving the desired behavior then it will invoke a greater sense of distress and lead to further emotional and behavioral problems.

While, in the opinion of the parent or teacher a reinforcement should be working, you cannot just assume that the reward is powerful enough to change the behavior. The only way you will know whether it is effective is if you see the results. Remember the child is OUR teacher. If it doesn't work, then you need to select a different reinforcement. A good strategy is to ask the child what they think will work for them.

Do not try to take on too much at one time. While these children may exhibit a number of problems, you will not be successful if you try to tackle every behavior at once. Set goals and prioritize where you think you are most likely to have the quickest success. It is just as important for you to feel successful as it is for you to be able to provide it for your child.

We have to be very clear that we understand the behavior that we are attempting to change. What is the cause? Where may it be coming from? What is sustaining it? Who may be driving it? Only by really looking at the behavior over time and in different settings can we get a clear impression of what is going on and what we may do about it.

In any plan, the most critical of all factors is how we administer the reinforcement. The most effective way to shape or increase the desired behavior is to reinforce it every time it occurs and reinforce it immediately. Too often we delay gratification or are not consistent or do not give it at all. At the onset, you need to provide the rewards immediately after you see the behavior.

To really see the change in the behavior, it is important to record the data. You usually do this by counting the frequency that it occurs. You measure it with the reinforcement. A recorded graph cannot lie. If the reinforcement is working the undesired behaviors will be decreasing.

At times we keep the same reward too long. What the child may want one day, he might not have any interest in the next. If you rely on just one or two things then the behavior may begin to deteriorate again. Talk with your child on a regular basis to find out what is motivating them. Of course, you can set limits on choices, but if you don't have anything that really motivates your child, chances are your program will not be successful.

If your child exhibits the desired behavior, in the plan, don't assume that that they will do it if you remove the consequence out of the plan. Consequences share two important functions. One is motivational and the other function is the feedback. What you need to build into the plan is a systematic and gradual reduction of the reinforcement.

Even if we agree that the child's behavior needs to change, that does not mean that we immediately start by applying direct consequences. The first thing we need to do is to make some outside changes first. That is, providing more support to see if the child has the initial skills to change. If not, then our intervention should be to show him/her the behavior and how to appropriately change it.

If a child is having a bad day due to fatigue, medication side effects, or events that may occur out of their control, continuing to discipline them will just frustrate them. Remember the many days that we have which start bad and just get worse. While there is some value in showing the child that "the show must go on," we may instead be teaching them that the world is uncaring and an uncompassionate place.

Motivation
Bringing out the best in your Child

Let's not underestimate ourselves, we can and do play crucial roles in awakening or developing the strengths within our children through the experiences you provide your child at home. Included here are some ways for you to bring out the best in your child, regardless of how he/she is packaged.

- Allow for your child to discover his/her own interests. Pay attention to the activities that they choose. There is a lot you can learn from this. Expose your child to a broad spectrum of experiences. This will activate skills, which perhaps neither you, nor they, knew about.

- Give permission for them to make mistakes. If they have to do things perfectly, they'll never take the risks necessary to make new discoveries about their world. Allow them to see that they are in control of the outcomes of their decisions.

- Allow them to see that they are in control of their behavior and that the consequences for appropriate behaviors are rewarded and poor behavior is disciplined. Teach them that they are not victims. Through this they learn the consequences of their decision-making. THESE ARE LIFE LESSONS!

- Plan special family projects. Shared creativity is known to awaken many new ideas and positive changes.

- Don't compare your child to anyone else and don't pressure them to be someone they are not. They will become inhibited, stressed and literally to exhausted to perform to your expectations. Allow your standards to be realistic.

- Keep your passions for learning and life ALIVE. Your child will learn from this.

- Don't criticize or judge the things that your child does. This destroys confidence and self-esteem.

- Share your success as a family, talk about good things that happened during the day, play with your child, show your sense of humor.

- Allow for your child to have a special place at home for them to play, work, dream and cry.

- Praise them... All the time and every day.

- Don't bribe your child.

- Teach your child to trust their intuition and believe in their abilities. Encourage them to try things that are different and maybe more difficult. Help them to confront their limitations with no shame. Help them confront their fears. Encourage them to keep on moving forward no matter what happens.

- ACCEPT YOUR CHILD FOR WHO THEY ARE!

Case Study 2

History - Alex is 91/2 years old and was professionally diagnosed as ADHD as well as oppositional defiance. He was referred as a result of his Mother's concern of poor school performance. He was extremely oppositional in the home setting and, he had difficulty with organizing himself.

His mother had a problem with structuring homework time for him. He was confused and angry due to his parents' marital separation and was plagued with an extremely poor self-esteem.

The first four years of his life were spent in day care where he experienced difficulty with change. He did not relate well to authority, did not listen and when he did not get his way, he went into tantrums. In his first grade, which was a dual language program, he was overwhelmed with the work and academic expectations and had just gone through a move when his parents separated. He had difficulty focusing and very often out of fear that he would not succeed he withdrew by running away and hiding in closets, under tables and desks.

He was placed on Ritalin by the pediatrician who diagnosed him as ADHD. On this medication, he was less anxious, focused better and showed some improvement in school. Although he scored above average in intelligence, he was an underachiever.

Second and third grades were average, but difficulty with structure was exhibited during the fourth grade.

He became more defiant, angry, withdrawn and non-compliant. His grades went below passing.

At that time the home was in chaos and very little control could be exerted by Mom or even Dad when he visited.

There was limited school support as they were not sure how to handle his behavior. The school was about to make the recommendation that he be retained in fourth grade.

Goals

- Defuse his defiant behavior.

- Increase level of success in school.

- To set limits for homework time, bedtime and argumentative behavior.

- Empower him by allowing him to see the results of his own decisions.

- Create a more positive relationship with his father.

- To show how Mom could empower herself through a greater awareness and shift of her parenting techniques.

Behavior Cycle

As an example, Alex would be watching television and Mom would ask him to turn it off and come to dinner, Alex would say, "okay mom, in two minutes". Mom would let it go and then ask again.

Alex would repeat, "okay mom, right away". This would go back and forth until mom would blow.

Alex learned that this was the way he could get attention from mom by being defiant.

Strategies

- Mom set up a behavior plan where she would give Alex one reminder. After that if he did not listen, he would have the consequence of losing a privilege. This was discussed with Alex beforehand so he was able to participate in the plan. The key here was Mom needed to take a stand, be consistent and follow through. This in effect was her major parenting shift.

- Mom met with the teacher to discuss strategies on how the curriculum could be modified for Alex to ensure greater success.

- Mom set up a communication system with Alex's teacher whereby they used his agenda book to pass notes back and forth.

- Mom set up a specific homework area for Alex. She specified what time he had to begin and that he had to complete his homework with 90% accuracy.

- Mom allowed Alex to make his behavioral decisions so that he would see that he was responsible for his own behavior or consequences and not be able to blame someone else.

- Mom set up regular family meetings between Dad, Alex and herself thereby allowing for Dad to participate in the process and showing Alex that Dad did have a stake in the outcome. This provided consistency throughout the family.

Results

- Alex's oppositional behavior was gone within three weeks.

- He became more compliant and more responsible for his behavior.

- He began to open up and was able to communicate his needs.

- He was generally less anxious and spent more quality time with Mom and Dad.

- The family was more supportive of one another.

- Alex proceeded to get better grades, he made new friends, was happier and had an increased self-esteem.

- Eventually he was withdrawn from the use of Ritalin and was retested and found to be misdiagnosed as ADHD.

In this case we see that Alex's ADHD was confused with emotional issues that created the same symptoms.

Working with your Shy-Withdrawn Child

If you consider your child to be shy and withdrawn it is most likely that they are quite sensitive, so that some extra care is required in being gentle with them.

Do not force or demand participation in activities, rather make the activity one that encourages your child's participation.

Engage them in tasks which seem to have potential for their interest and which require interaction.

Have your child help you with some task or game. Give them some responsibilities that you are sure that they can handle.

Give concrete, tangible rewards as well as liberal praise and encouragement as your child begins to make progress.

Role-play situations where the child can try out more assertive behaviors. The more practice they get the bolder their behavior will be.

Work with a lot of storytelling and use imaginary stories where the child may role-play a favorite character.

Sometimes role-playing certain situations where your child is feeling uncomfortable will help to dissipate it or help you understand it better. For example, how to act and what to say when trying to make new friends. Role-play situations that may occur in the park or at a party. Teach them how to approach someone new on the block.

Ask them and talk about:

- How they make friends?
- What is a friend to them?
- What do they feel makes a good friend?
- What it means to take risks?

Summary of Helpful hints

Slow down, step back and take a long look at your world.

Look at yourselves and the role that you are playing in the life of your child.

Include yourselves in the plan. Observe necessary changes and make the adjustments.

Allow your child to see that they are in control of their outcomes. From this they will learn the consequences of their good decision making vs. poor decision making. They are learning life's lessons.

Teach them that they are not victims, and that they are responsible for their own behavior.

It is the role of a parent to allow their child to learn from within and not be afraid to assert themselves. Help and encourage them to feel confident and secure.

Be involved and aware of what is going on in your child's head, heart and school.

Praise their efforts.

Remember that mistakes are opportunities for growth and learning.

Be consistent, be firm and be caring.

Managing Homework Time

I believe every parent will agree that family stress levels increase during homework time and continue as the dinner and then bedtime hour approaches. Does it feel at times that you are preparing to do battle with seemingly no ammunition! Homework is often the major cause of family battles - not to be won - but the cause of tremendous chaos.

Homework should be a means of practicing previously taught material, so if your children cannot do it, this may be an indication that something is going wrong and it would be a good time to set up a meeting with their teacher.

The following recommendations will minimize some of the stress associated with homework time:

Exercise will assist your child in his ability to stay focused. Have them engage in some form of challenging exercise program approximately 20 minutes prior to starting their homework.

At the elementary level, it should be completed before dinner. Allow for a 30-minute break after school as snack time and a winding down period before getting started. Following the same routine and time pattern everyday is important.

Designate specific areas for homework and studying. Possibilities include the child's room or the kitchen or dining room table. If you have a basement, you may want to create a special work area. Eliminate as much distraction as possible. Be sure that there is sufficient space to spread out materials. A table that allows for all necessary supplies such as pencils, pens, paper and books works well. Place a bulletin board in your child's workspace. Keeping supplies on hand is important. Check with your child and teacher about their needs.

Try to ignore off task behavior. Sit down with your child and set up goals outlining your expectations and the consequences. Then remember to follow through. Inconsistencies in following the plan will just increase the exact behaviors that you are trying to eliminate.

If your child maintains an agenda book, have the teacher initial it upon satisfactory completion. You initial it as well. Call the teacher every two weeks or so to make sure things are on track. If assignments are too difficult, write notes to the teacher. Keep an extra set of schoolbooks on hand to be prepared for the times when they are forgotten.

Get a large calendar, one that allows space for jotting down notes and reminders in the daily boxes. Tear off two or three months at a time and post them in your child's work area. Mark in test dates, projects and reports that are due. Once your child gets into a routine to check the calendar this will be an excellent reminder and help him with time management.

Check to make sure that your child understands the assignments. Keep a record as to when your child begins; the actual time spent doing it and the time of completion. These 3 things will provide a good indicator if problems do exist and if things are improving or not.

The key to success is to follow your management system. Your caring, firm, gentle and consistent attitude will play an important role in determining the results.

Teenagers - ADHD or Not

After all of this talk on behavior management techniques, role playing and token reinforcements for your elementary age child, I bet you were asking when we would get to your teenager. Well we both know that teenagers are a special entity on to themselves so we are about to give them their due.

While hormones, the struggle for independence and an emerging identity are wreaking havoc both on you and your teenager, the main issue is how much freedom to give, how much "attitude" to take, what kind of disciplines to use and what issues are worth fighting about. But even with all of this, setting up behavior plans, being consistent and firm remains the focus of your relationship.

To guide your teenager to adulthood and help negotiate relationships, setting goals and supporting values is quite a journey. You may not be able to anticipate some of the landmines, but the trick is to learn and see what works best for both your child and yourself. One of the challenges is to find a way to keep the road open between you and them so that as those landmines erupt, you will be in a better position to "chill" until cooler heads prevail.

For your teenager this is a time to test out their independence, to take risks, to be extremely self-centered and self-focused. They know everything and do not want to hear any advice coming from your direction. Lectures in many cases are just a waste of time and energy. They are beginning to make decisions on their own and these decisions are indications of the path they are choosing. Now, no matter what the results of these decisions (excluding the cases where they can get themselves into some serious trouble) they should be encouraged to think for themselves. They are in the process of fine-tuning the skills, which you have guided them by, and preparing for adulthood. So even though the changes that are occurring often seem confusing and challenging, it can also be a very rewarding experience as you have a front seat view of your child going out into the world and becoming who they really are.

Although teenagers will make their own choices, a good home life can increase the odds that kids will avoid some of the pitfalls of adolescence. Passive listening works well. A kind warm and open relationship. One, which demonstrates respect for one another, will set a reassuring tone and at the same time you will be teaching them to be understanding, open and caring. The key here is to balance this with setting firm boundaries.

There are three major areas that are important to the development of your relationship with your teenager.

These are connection, observation and supervision and we can throw in freedom for good measure.

First, a close connection and understanding between yourself and your child provides a basis for the entire relationship. If your connection is consistent, positive, warm, open and stable, your child is more likely to take this into their outside world. Their social interactions and decisions will reflect this. They are more likely to respond to others positively and with compassion and understanding and to have a healthy self-esteem and attract others to them with this attribute.

In addition to developing a close connection between yourself and your adolescent, it is important to observe when they may require supervision. Research indicates that teenagers really enjoy when their parents take a keen interest in their activities, even though at times they may not show it. Teens whose parents know who their friends are and what they do in their free time are less likely to get into trouble. In the context of a warm, kind relationship this observation and supervision of your child's activities comes across as caring rather than being nosy and intrusive.

Your teenager will love it when you encourage them to experience some degree of their freedom. This should be nurtured in children. Encouraging independent thinking and expression of one's beliefs and unconditional love will promote a greater sense of autonomy in your child. The lesson here is not to control our children or try to make them into clones of ourselves.

If you wish to enrich your connection with your teenager find activities which you both enjoy doing together. Not only are you spending quality and fun time together, but you are also teaching honesty, trust, sportsmanship, and respect for each other, which are crucial attributes for effective disciplining. When necessary it will be required that you enforce consequences when rules and limits are broken. By staying on top of it and following through you will most definitely save yourself the heartache later on.

We need to remember that the motivating force of ALL teenagers is the necessity to challenge their freedom. They will not let you know that they feel more secure and in control when they know that you are setting firm boundaries for them. The limits that you set, believe it or not, actually provide a sense of stability in teens while they are struggling to understand relationships and the roles that they play in their community.

One of the major challenges that we as parents have is the disciplining of our teenagers. If you were to include your child in establishing rules about appropriate behavior/limits and their consequences, much of the tension and disagreements would probably end. Once this has been accomplished then the responsibility belongs to them. Your role becomes one of calmly enforcing the pre-arranged consequence. This then becomes an opportunity for them to evaluate what decisions they have made and make any necessary adjustments. Helping to set the rules may not stop your teenager from breaking the rule, but it will help you to avoid power struggles with them.

A very common trap that we fall into is attempting to control our kids, believing that if we control what they think that this will translate into our wishful behavior for them. So quite often we will shut them out, withdraw attention, and invalidate their beliefs or use guilt and shame. This actually creates a greater separation between our parent/child relationships. In addition, without knowing it, we are teaching them how to duplicate these behaviors in their everyday social activities. This will in turn show up in their other interactions and in their parenting style later on in life.

To Summarize

In your relationship with your teenager it is important to:

- Pay attention when they talk.

- Watch as well as listen. Learn to know when they need you and when they don't.

- Do not take things personally when you are getting "attitude" from them. We often see this as a lack of respect.

- Try not to interrupt when it is their turn to speak.

- Re-phrase his/her words, to be sure you understand them and that they understand you.

- If you don't have time to listen at the moment, set a time when it is convenient for both.

- It is okay to disagree, but disagree with respect for one another.

- Respect your child's feelings. Do not dismiss them. You may not always be able to help but they will know that you are there with your support and love.

- Yes of course you will get angry, but do it rationally and in a calm way. Do it in a way that you are teaching them about their decisions. Stay away from character assassinations that become very disempowering.

- Channel your discussions towards solving problems. Be willing to negotiate and compromise. These are everyday life lessons taught in a healthy and open way.

- When rules are broken, GO AHEAD and follow through. Don't be afraid to be unpopular for a day or two. Believe it or not, all children see the setting of healthy limits as a form of caring.

- Let your child be the teenager they want to be, not the one you wish them to be.

- Don't be afraid to share with them that you have made a mistake and apologize when necessary.

The common theme to all of the above is to communicate with your teen. Communication comes in all different forms, by talking, by listening, by watching and sometimes by just knowing not to say anything at all.

CHAPTER 12

Conclusion

Introspective Thoughts

In writing this work, I had an opportunity to re-experience many aspects of my own life. I have spent over 20 years working with children and families as a teacher, principal, advocate, family counselor and parent although not necessarily in that order. Like you I have gone through the confusion, fears and joys of having a family, experiencing the ups and downs, the guilt and the anger. I have spent countless hours as a teacher trying to figure out the answers for my students who were going through the same frustrations and joys as your children do. As a principal, not only did I again experience these same feelings, but I had the opportunity to counsel teachers as they went through their day dealing with these same issues. In all of this I can say with all my being that I loved the moments I spent with you, talking through the good times and bad, the strengths and weaknesses of your children and what to do or not to do when faced with difficult decisions. As a family counselor, working with you right in your home, for me this is the ultimate experience. It has allowed me to see the whole picture, and it allows me to help you create a new picture for you and your child. A picture that does not negate the tears, anger and frustration, but embraces it all and focuses on ways to adjust that picture by looking at different aspects of your life and altering those aspects to create a new paradigm.

One of the most glaring observations I have made is, that as an outsider it is easy to make recommendations, suggestions and even judgements as to what to do with your kids, changes that need to be made, things that could have, or should have been done differently. But it all comes back to one thing, and that is that for you as the parents who are living, breathing, and sleeping with these challenges day in and day out there is no break and certainly there is no simple answer. One day goes into the next, time just flies by and it seems as if everything is a crisis, nothing is going right and that there will never be a peaceful end to this experience.

Yes, at times it really does seem that life is full of negativity and that there is no way out of this maze. So why read another self-help book or have to listen to someone who calls himself an authority on parenting?

I see now that it was my journey that allowed for me to share all of this information with you. It is my passion and dedication that has allowed me to endure bringing "There is No Magic" to you. That this book is indeed all about me and all about you and the experiences we have shared. I offer myself as a very humble role model. Living proof that no matter how difficult change may be and that, no matter how bleak things may look, there is always room for a positive outlook, and with this change of attitude brings change of feelings, which ultimately brings changes in behavior.

For some it may not seem so but, "There is No Magic", is more than a guide and a bunch of details and information. It was written with the objective of allowing you, the parent, to have an opportunity to become a better teacher, advocate, and counselor for your child.

To help you realize that as a parent you need to take a greater responsibility in the total education of your child.

So yes indeed let's not negate that our child and family are in crisis, that our school budgets and educational programming are dwindling and that things are seemingly even more chaotic. Why not use this as our platform to move forward, STEP by STEP and reintroduce the value of commitment to our sons and daughters, commitment to work diligently to achieve set goals?

Let us choose a path that allows for our children to explore their own unique creativity and vocation. A path that encourages and enhances their inherent strengths and gifts and allows them the freedom to explore and be creative. Give them the chance, support and tools to be the absolute best they can be, our future geniuses. We can not afford to leave this to chance and happenstance.

Let us work as partners with our children so as to promote positive growth from within our children and from within ourselves.

When we can accomplish this change in attitude towards the upbringing of our child, we will truly see, that the magic is, that ...

THERE IS NO MAGIC

BIBLIOGRAPHY

American Psychiatric Association (1994), *Diagnostic and statistical manual of mental disorders* (4th ed., rev.) (DSM-1V-R)., Washington, D.C: APA

Barkley et al., as cited in Fowler, M. (1992) *The C.H.A.D.D. educator's Manual.* Plantation Fl. Children and Adults with Attention Deficit Disorder.

Barkley, R.D., New ways of looking at ADHD (lecture 1991) Third annual C.H.A.D.D. conference on attention deficit disorders. Washington D.C.

Baumrind, D. (1991). " The influence of parenting style on adolescent competence and substance abuse." *Journal of Early Adolescence.* 11 (1), 56-95

Blank, R., & Remschmidt, H., "Hyperkinetic Syndrome: The Role of Allergy Among Psychological and Neurological Factors." *European Child and Adolescent Psychiatry,* (1994), 3(4), pp. 220-228.

Bradway, K. (1964. "Jung's Psychological Types," *Journal of Analytical Psychology,* vol.9. Tavistock Publishers. Pp.129-135.

Burgess, J., et al., "Long Chain Polyunsaturated Fatty Acids in Children with Attention deficit Hyperactivity Disorder," *American Journal of Clinical Nutrition,* (2000), 63 (1-2), pp. 79-87.

Business Week Magazine. (Feb. 1994). *Computers as teacher and tutor.*

Carter, M., et al., "Effects of a Few Foods Diet in Attention Deficit Disorder," *Archives of Disease in Childhood,* (1993), 69, pp. 564-568.

Day, Charlene., (2001), *Body Basics*, Potentials Within.

Department of Education., Government of Western Australia. (2001)

Edwards, G. (1995) Book reviews: Attention deficits and hyperactivity in children (1994), by Stephen P. Hinshaw. *ADHD Report,* 3(1), p. 13.

Erasmus, Udo. *Fats that Heal, Fats that Kill.* Burnaby B.C. Canada: Alive Books, (1993).

Eric Digest #459., Washington D.C.

Ewin, Jeannette. *The Fats We Need to Eat. Essential fatty Acids. Feeling healthy, Looking Young.* London: Thorsons (1995)

Ginott, H.G. (1993). *Teacher and Child: A Book for Parents and Teachers,* N.Y. pp: 112, 126, 152.

Glass, J. (1974). *Glass Analysis,* New York, N.Y.

Goodyear, P. & Hynd, G.W. (1992). "Behavioral & Neuropsychological differentiation., *Journal of Clinical Psychology, 21.* pp. 273-305.

Hills, Sandra, N.D. & Wyman, P. *What's Food Got to do with it? Natural Remedies for learning Disabilities.* Windsor, Ca.: The Center for New Discoveries in Learning. (1997)

Ingersoll, B. (1988). *Your hyperactive child.* New York: Doubleday.

Jin, P. (1992) " Efficacy of Tai Chi, brisk walking, meditation and reading in reducing mental and emotional stress." *Journal of Psychosomatic Research.* 36: pp. 361-370.

Jung, C. (1923). *Psychological Types.,* New York. Harcourt Brace.

Khalsa, P., & Karta, S. "Keeping Children Healthy," *Yoga Journal.* (Oct. 1996)

Kiersey, D., & Bates, M., (1978). *Please Understand Me. Character and Temperament Types.* Prometheus Nemesis Book Company, Delmor, Ca.

Kreger-Silverman, Linda Ph.D., Gifted Development Center, Institute for the study of advanced development. Denver, Co. (1997)

Miller, N.B., Cowan, P.A., Cowan C.P., & Hetherington, E.M. (1993). "Externalizing in pre-schoolers and early adolescents. A cross study replication of a family model. *Developmental Psychology, 29* (1), 3-18

National Institute of Mental Health, *Laureate Saint Francis Hospital.* Washington. DC.

Office of Mental Retardation (OMRDD)., Albany, N.Y.

Onkka, Timothy Ph.D. Director, Alpha Center, Northern Indiana School of Psychology

Pelligrini, A., & Horvat, M. (1995) A developmental contextualist critique of attention deficit hyperactivity disorder. *Educational Researcher, 24*(1), 13-19.

Physicians' Desk reference (1995)., Thomson Healthcare, Montvale, N.J.

Pruitt K.S., & Dornbush, P.M. (1995). *Teaching the Tiger, A handbook for individuals involved in the education of students with attention deficit disorders, Tourette syndrome or obsessive-compulsive disorder.*

Reeve, R. (1994) The Academic impact of ADHD. *Attention,* 1(1) pp.8-12

Richardson, A.J., McDaid, A.M., Calvin, C.M. et al. "Reduced behavioral and learning problems in children with specific learning difficulties after supplementation with highly unsaturated fatty acids: a randomized, double blind, placebo controlled trial." Federation of Neuroscience Societies. Brighton, U.K.

Robleda, Johanna, S., Special Projects Director, *The Parent Center.* San Francisco, Ca. (1997)

Rossi, R., & Montgomery, A. (1994) Becoming at risk of failure in America's schools. In Rossi, R., & Montgomery, A. (Eds.), *Educational reforms and students at risk: A review of the current state of the art (pp 1-45).* Washington DC: Office of Research, United States Department of Education.

Royal National Institute of the Blind. (June 1998)., Peterborough, England.

Scadding, G., & Brostoff, J. "Immunological Responses to Food." In J. Hunter and D. Jones (Eds.), *Food and the Gut,* Philadelphia: Saunders, 1985, pp. 94-112.

Schmidt, M., *Smart fats. How Dietary Fats and Oils affect Mental, Physical and Emotional Intelligence.* Berkely, Ca.: (1997)

Sequence of reading & Math skills, taken from research and handout material prepared by: The Child School. New York, N.Y.

Smith-Taylor, L., "Dance and ADD – A heartwarming story of how dance positively impacted the lives of one family living with ADHD. (1995)

Stordy, J., & Nicholl, J.M. *The LCP Solution: The Remarkable Nutritional Treatment for ADHD, Dyslexia & Dyspraxia (2000) Random House, New York.*

Sumar, S., *Yoga for the Special Child,* (1996)

The Baby Center, "The Visual Learner." (1997)

The Council for Exceptional Children, " Special Education Administrative Policies Manual."(1977)

The Nalanda Institute., Mumbai, India. (2000)

USA Today Weekend Edition (October, 1995)

Under the Rainbow, " A Parents' Guide to Learning Disabilities., A publication of the Learning Disabilities Association of Toronto.

Ward, N., " Assessment of Chemical Factors in relation to Child Hyperactivity," *Journal of Nutritional and Environmental Medicine,* (1997), 7, pp. 333-342.

Weiss, L.H. & Schwarz, J.C. (1996). "The relationship between parenting types and older adolescents' personality, academic achievement, adjustment and substance abuse. *Child Development.* 67 (5), 2101-2114

Weiss & Hechtman, as cited in Fowler, M. (1992). *The C.H.A.D.D. educator's manual.* Plantation Fl. Children and Adults with Attention Deficit Disorder.

Wendt, M., "How Running and Exercise can Impact the Behavior of ADHD Children." *Stay Fit and Healthy with Kids Running.* (Jan. 2001).

Wolfson, L., Whipple, R., Derby, C., Judge, J., King, M., Amerman, P., Schmidt, J., & Smyers, D. (1996). " Balance and strength training in older adults: intervention gains and Tai Chi maintenance." *Journal of American Geriatrics Society.* 44(5) pp. 498-506.

Zentall, S. (1993). Research on educational implications of attention deficit hyperactivity disorder. *Exceptional Children,* 60(2), pp. 143-153.

Zimmerman, M., C.N. *The ADD Nutrition Solution. A Drug Free- 30 day Plan.* New York: Holt & Company 1999.

NATIONAL ORGANIZATIONS

Children and Adults with Attention Deficit Disorder (CH.A.D.D.)
8181 Professional Place, Suite 201
Landover, Md. 20785
(800) 233-4050

Council for Exceptional Children
1920 Association Dr.
Reston, Va. 22091-1589
(703) 620-3660

Council for Learning Disabilities
P.O. Box 40303
Overland, Ks. 66204
(913) 492-8755

Educational Resources Information Center (ERIC)
1920 Association Dr.
Reston, Va. 22091-1589
(800) 328-0272

International Dyslexia Association
Chester Building, Suite 382
8600 La Salee Road
Baltimore, Md. 21286-2044
(800) 222-3123

Learning Disability Association of America
4156 Library Road
Pittsburgh, Pa. 15234
(412) 341-1515

National Association of Private Schools for Exceptional Children
1522 K Street, NW Suite1032
Washington, DC 20005
(202) 408-3338

Related Organizations:

American Speech-Language-Hearing Association
10801 Rockville Pike
Rockville, MD 20852
(800) 638-8255

Asperger Syndrome Coalition of the United States
P.O. Box 2577
Jacksonville, Fl. 32203-2577

Association of Educational Therapists
1804 W. Burbank Blvd.
Burbank, Ca. 91506
(818) 843-1183

Developmental Delay Resources
6701 Fairfax Road
Chevy Chase, MD 20815
(301) 652-2263

National Association for the Education of Young Children
1509 16th Street, NW
Washington, DC 20036-1426
(800) 424-2460

National Association of School Psychologists
4340 East-West Highway   Suite 402
Bethesda, Md. 20814
(301) 657-0270

National Association for Rare Disorders
P.O. Box 8923
New Fairfield, Ct. 06812-8923
(800) 999-6673

Recording for The Blind and Dyslexic
20 Roszol Road

Princeton, New Jersey 08540
(800) 221-4792

Zero to Three
National Center for Infants, Toddlers and Families
734 15th St., NW   Suite 1000
Washington, DC 20005
(202) 638-1144

Advocacy & Legal Issues:

Council of Parent Attorneys and Advocates
P.O. Box 81-7327
Hollywood, Fl. 33081-0327
(954) 966-4489

National Center for Law and Learning Disabilities
P.O. Box 368
Cabin John, MD 20818
(301) 469-8308